Critical Acclaim For Books by Gen and Kelly Tanabe

Authors of *Adult Students: A Painless Guide to Going Back to College,
The Ultimate Scholarship Book* and *Get Free Cash for College*

"Upbeat, well-organized and engaging, this comprehensive tool is an exceptional investment."
—*Publishers Weekly*

"Helpful, well-organized guide, with copies of actual letters and essays and practical tips. A good resource for all students."
—*KLIATT*

"Upbeat tone and clear, practical advice."
—*Book News*

"What's even better than all the top-notch tips is that the book is written in a cool, conversational way."
—*College Bound Magazine*

"A 'must' for any prospective college student."
—*Midwest Book Review*

"Invaluable information ranging from the elimination of admission myths to successfully tapping into scholarship funds."
—Leonard Banks, *The Journal Press*

"The Tanabes literally wrote the book on the topic."
—*Bull & Bear Financial Report*

"Offers advice on writing a good entrance essay, taking exams and applying for scholarships and other information on the college experience—start to finish."
—*Town & Country Magazine*

501 Ways for Adult Students to Pay for College

Gen and Kelly Tanabe

Award-winning authors of *Adult Students: A Painless Guide to Going Back to College, The Ultimate Scholarship Book* and *Get Free Cash for College*

501 Ways for Adult Students to Pay for College (6th Edition)
By Gen and Kelly Tanabe

Published by SuperCollege, LLC
2713 Newlands Avenue, Belmont, CA 94002 | 650-618-2221 | www.supercollege.com

Credits: Additional research by Rita Cook. Cover design by TLC Graphics. Illustrations by Terry Smith (www.t-smith.org). Back cover photo by Alvin Gee (www.alvingee.com).

Trademarks: All brand names, product names and services used in this book are trademarks, registered trademarks or tradenames of their respective holders. SuperCollege is not associated with any college, university, product or vendor.

Disclaimers: The authors and publisher have used their best efforts in preparing this book. It is sold with the understanding that the authors and publisher are not rendering legal, accounting, investment, tax or other professional advice. The reader must seek the services of a qualified professional for such advice. The authors and publisher cannot be held responsible for any loss incurred as a result of specific financial, tax or investment planning decisions made by the reader. The authors and publisher make no representations or warranties with respect to the accuracy or completeness of the contents of the book and specifically disclaim any implied warranties or merchantability or fitness for a particular purpose. The accuracy and completeness of the information provided herein and the opinions stated herein are not guaranteed or warranted to produce any particular results. The authors and publisher specifically disclaim any responsibility for any liability, loss or risk, personal or otherwise, which is incurred as a consequence, directly or indirectly, of the use and application of any of the contents of this book.

ISBN 978-1-61760-126-2

Manufactured in the United States of America
10 9 8 7 6 5 4 3 2 1

Library of Congress Cataloging-in-Publication Data
Tanabe, Gen S.
 501 ways for adult students to pay for college : going back to school without going broke / Gen Tanabe, Kelly Tanabe.
     pages cm
 Includes index.
 Summary: "With information on online and part-time classes and new financial aid, loan, and scholarship opportunities, this updated resource teaches adult students how to find and win scholarships, get financial aid for online programs, receive larger financial aid packages, take advantage of educational tax breaks, and cancel education debts with loan forgiveness programs"-- Provided by publisher.
 ISBN 978-1-61760-126-2 (pbk.)
 1. Student aid--United States--Handbooks, manuals, etc. 2. Student aid--United States--Directories. 3. Scholarships--United States--Handbooks, manuals, etc. 4. Scholarships--United States--Directories. 5. College costs--United States. 6. Adult college students. I. Tanabe, Kelly Y. II. Title. III. Title: Five hundred one ways for adult students to pay for college. IV. Title: Five hundred and one ways for adult students to pay for college.
 LB2337.4.T355 2017
 378.30973--dc23
                                              2014036275

CONTENTS AT A GLANCE

TABLE OF CONTENTS

We dedicate this book to you and the hundreds of thousands of adults each year who are courageously going back to school to fulfill personal and professional dreams.

We hope that this book will help you make your dreams of higher education a little more affordable.

Get the Money You Need

Get The Money You Need

Congratulations on your decision to go back to school. Believe it or not, you are now part of the fastest-growing population on college campuses. Today more than three million students over the age of 35 are in college pursuing both professional and personal dreams.

While education is known to "free the mind," education itself is anything but free. Unlike a teenager fresh out of high school, you don't have the luxury of parental support, college counselors to guide you through applying for financial aid and easy-to-find scholarships. Plus, with families to support and mortgage payments, paying for college takes on a whole new level of complexity.

But we suspect that you already know this and are determined to go back to school despite the costs. That's where this book can help. In *501 Ways for Adult Students to Pay for College* you will learn valuable strategies that will help you get the money you need to pay for your education. We'll also show you resources that can make your education affordable. And we'll do it in a jargon-free manner that is easy to understand and that you can quickly put into action.

How This Book Will Help You Cut Your Tuition Bill

501 Ways for Adult Students to Pay for College covers nearly every conceivable way to pay for college. The following is just a small sampling of what you will learn:

Find scholarships just for adults. Banish the thought that scholarships are only for high school students. You will be amazed at how many awards there are for adult students. The key is to know where to look. We'll show you how to use your past career experience, future career goals, academic interests, hobbies and interests to find scholarships. We'll also give you a list of scholarships that are aimed specifically at adult students.

Tap into resources from your employer. While you may not have parents who can foot the tuition bill, you just might have an employer who is willing to help. We'll show you various deals that you can make with your employer to pay for tuition. We also have a great story of an adult student who was able to successfully negotiate with his employer to pay for his education.

Turn work and life experience into actual college credit. You can cut years off of your education (and therefore save $$$ on tuition) by convincing the college that your work and life experiences are worth college credit. We'll give you the low down on the various exams, portfolios and petitions that you can use to get credit.

Federal and state financial aid programs. Financial aid should be a part of every student's strategy to get money for college. We take the mystery out of the various financial aid programs and show you what you may qualify for as well as what restrictions you may encounter.

Get Uncle Sam to help. You pay a lot in taxes, and it's only fair that you get some of this back in the form of federal retraining programs and child care and education grants. There are also important tax breaks for adult students.

Go to school without giving up work. There are many part-time and online programs that allow you to continue to earn an income while earning a degree. You may even find that a much less expensive certificate program is all you need to advance your career. We'll cover each option and show you both the advantages and disadvantages.

How To Read This Book

There is no "right way" to pay for college. After reading this book we know you'll be surprised at how many different ways there are to make your education affordable. The best way to read this book is to start with the introduction of each chapter and flip through some of the specific strategies. As you are reading you should feel that great "Ah-ha" when you find a way that you can use in your own situation. Jot the number down and keep reading. By exposing yourself to the many ways that you can pay for school you'll be sure to find a certain number that are right for you.

In our research we have found that the most common cause of stress and hardship among adult students is that they are simply unaware of the various ways to pay for school. Or they have a vague notion (such as "I gotta find a scholarship") of what they need to do but don't have real examples and resources to know where to start. *501 Ways for Adult Students to Pay for College* will give you both the variety of opportunities and the detailed understanding to be able to create your own opportunities.

Our no-nonsense approach extends even to the way we have chosen to organize this book. As the title suggests, we have grouped the countless ways that you can pay for tuition into a manageable set of 501 ways. We have further divided these ways into easy-to-digest chapters. We have gone to great lengths to make sure that we give you both general strategies and specific resources. In our chapter on scholarships, for example, we'll show you how to find scholarships in your own community. At the same time we will also give you a list of specific scholarships just for adults. Our goal is to save you time by giving you as much specific information as possible while also showing you the larger picture so that you can go out and find opportunities on your own.

During the research of this book we met hundreds of wonderful adults, like you, who have gone back to school. Listening to their stories we realized that they not only illustrate the various ways that you can pay for your education but they are also incredibly inspirational. We have included some of their stories throughout the book. When you read them you will realize that you are not alone in the challenges that you face. In fact, countless other adults have gone before, faced similar challenges and ultimately devised ways to overcome them. We are sure that you will find these stories both informative and entertaining.

What Are You Waiting For? Let's Get Started!

We had more fun writing this and our other book, *Adult Students: An Insider's Guide to Getting Into College* than many of our other books. The reason is because adult students are very different than typical college students. Think back to when you were 17 or 18 years old. Most of us took everything in our life at that age for granted. We took for granted that we would be going to college. Or maybe that someday we would go to college. We took for granted the help that our parents and teachers were willing to give to send us to school. But for everything that a teenager takes for granted, an adult student is acutely aware of and appreciates.

Adults know the importance of an education. Adults are aware of the costs and sacrifices it takes to go to school and never miss an opportunity to take advantage of what their colleges offer. Adults know that their education is the one asset that will improve their lives more than anything else–including money. It is for these reasons that colleges love adult students–and so do we.

It has been such an inspiration for us to meet the 30-, 40-, 50- and 60-something men and women who are making the ultimate sacrifice of jobs and material comfort to go back to college. We have seen the energy and effort that is involved in making this transition and we hope that by writing this book we can help those readers who are contemplating taking the plunge to do so with a little less worry.

We have seen the tremendous personal and professional satisfaction that students get from completing their educations. While such an achievement is indeed priceless, we are committed to making that goal as inexpensive and downright as cheap as it can possibly be.

So, find a comfortable chair. Grab a highlighter. And read on to find out how you, too, can make your dream of going to school possible.

The Best Places to Find Scholarships for Adults

Extra! Adult Student Scholarships Do Exist!

For many adults the word "scholarship" is somewhat of a tease. You know there are scholarships out there and you've heard stories of the vast amount of free dollars just waiting to be claimed. But when you try to find specific scholarships to apply to you feel lost. Where are all these scholarships? Even more frustrating is when you do come across a scholarship more often than not it's for a 17-year-old high schooler and not a 20-, 30-, 40- or (God forbid) 50-something student.

Having dreams of free scholarship dollars cruelly dashed by reality, most adults simply give up and look for other ways to pay.

Don't let this happen to you.

The reality is there **are** scholarships for adults. Adult student scholarships are not a myth, mirage or pipe dream. They are real, and you can find them. All you need to know is where to look.

Reality Check

Before we start looking for scholarships we need to acknowledge one important fact: the majority of resources, including books and websites, are geared toward high school students. Therefore, if you use these resources (and you most definitely should) you will obviously find many more scholarships for teens than for adults.

Don't be discouraged.

When you start your scholarship search, expect that the easiest scholarships to find will be for teenagers. This does not mean that there aren't any good scholarships for adults. It just means that you'll have to look harder and be more creative in where you search to dig up awards that you may apply to win.

There's another reason not to be discouraged. Having a lack of websites and scholarship books just for adults is not necessarily a bad thing. Even for high school students the vast majority who actually win scholarships usually find these awards through their own detective work. The problem with having many easy-to-find scholarships is that it doesn't encourage you to be selective about which ones to apply to. Many students waste their time applying to dozens of scholarships that they find easily on a website without taking the time to really match the awards to their background, interests or future goals. In addition, many students only use the Internet or printed scholarship directories for their scholarship search. While websites and books cite impressive statistics about how many scholarships they have, the reality is that they are still indexing only a small fraction of the total scholarships that are out there.

To find scholarships that you have the best chance of winning you are going to need to do your own detective work. There are no shortcuts. But by doing so you will be able to not only find more awards but also awards that really fit your background and goals, which will dramatically increase your odds of winning.

Lena's Story

On the outside Lena Nsomeka-Gomes, 39, lived a comfortable life. She had a steady job in a clinic where she had worked her way up from being an HIV counselor to a case manager. Lena lived in a nice apartment and had plenty of free time, which she spent with friends and doing the things she enjoyed. But inside Lena felt something was missing. That something was professional satisfaction, which she knew would only come from going back to school.

"I got burned out in my job because I realized it was a dead end. I had gone as far as I could go and just got tired of the endless rut I was in," she admits. While some people would have just accepted the situation, Lena decided to do something about it and made the bold decision to go back to school. This time she would finally be able to earn her degree at a profession she had loved all her life. "I wanted to write," she says. "I have always written on the side. I wanted to change my life completely and do what I always dreamed of doing: finish college and accomplish something big."

Lena's decision had far-reaching consequences that went beyond her personal finances. As Lena explains, her job had come to define her. "Giving up my job meant giving up a part of my identity. Going back to school was like taking off a mask and standing naked in a hallway without mirrors. I was scared and didn't know if I had what it would take to endure three years of college successfully," she confesses.

But if fear kept Lena up at night, it was her determination that got her through the challenges. Her first step was to open a separate savings account dedicated to her goal. "I began to dump in extra money when I had it," she explains. Lena also chose to first attend a less-expensive community college where she spent $40 per class instead of $300 at a regular university. After completing her basic requirements at the community college she transferred to San Francisco State University to complete her BA in journalism.

While community college was affordable, once she got to S.F. State her costs skyrocketed. Lena first applied for financial aid but was disqualified because she had outstanding student loans that were in default from years earlier. "I knew my only source of financial aid would have to come from private scholarships," she recalls.

She began an exhaustive search for scholarships. Like many students Lena started with the Internet and applied for every award that she was eligible for and diligently followed the application instructions. As a result of her efforts Lena received two "hefty" scholarships, one of which was the *Jeanette Rankin Foundation Adult Scholarship Award*. The money from these two scholarships covered her tuition, books and supplies.

Lena strongly encourages every adult student to look for scholarships. "There are literally thousands of scholarships available for non-traditional students," she explains. On why more adults don't take advantage of these opportunities, Lena feels that the main problem is that students "don't manage their time well enough." While understandable considering how busy most are it stills means that many adults are passing up free money.

Lena understands how hard it is to make time to apply for a scholarship that you don't know if you will win. "It takes time to apply," she says, explaining that you have to fill out applications, get letters of recommendations and usually write a personal essay of about 500 to 1,000 words. She says you must begin the research and writing process well in advance and recommends at least six months before you start school. In her case, she searched for scholarships on the Internet and in books that she got from the library and bookstore. She applied to eight scholarships, which took her about two months of work. She was awarded two and is still waiting to hear from more.

There's another advantage of scholarships, according to Lena. "The great thing about scholarships is that many of them are not just tuition based. In other words, you can pay your car insurance and your rent—anything to keep you in school. The only thing you must do is make sure to keep all of your receipts because when you do your taxes the IRS will want to know how you spent that money," says Lena.

Lena's advice to all adult students who have to pay for college is not to rely only on financial aid. Although federal and state governments are able to defray some costs, she says you can end up taking out too many loans to make up the differences. "That's why I can't emphasize enough how important it is to look for scholarships," she says.

While her life has changed dramatically since she began attending school, Lena believes that "money gained or lost cannot compare to the fulfillment of realizing your dreams." Working on her degree has increased her confidence while at the same time helped to build her academic and writing skills.

"I have never been this happy," she says. "My family and friends have stood by my side waving and cheering me on. I feel phenomenal." Lena's plans for the future include reporting for a newspaper and a wire service as well as venturing into media relations and eventually writing books.

The Golden Rule Of Scholarships

As an adult you'll find that there are two major types of scholarships. The first are scholarships specifically for adult students. There are a number of scholarships for "non-traditional" or "returning" students. These have specific requirements that exclude "traditional" students such as an age minimum or requiring that applicants have taken a break from school to raise a family or work. The second are scholarships aimed at any student who is in college regardless of whether they are "traditional" or "non-traditional." These scholarships are far more numerous and usually require that you are in a specific year of study such as a freshman in college or that you pursue a particular major. Scholarships that are open to college freshmen are also the ones that you'll apply to before you actually start school. Most of these scholarships let you apply before you actually begin so that you can use the money to pay for your first year in school. These scholarships typically don't have an age limit and therefore you will be competing against not only other adult students but also traditional students.

It's this second type of scholarship that most adults don't consider because they are not specifically directed at adult students. But if you ignore these you will be leaving a ton of money on the table.

Thus, the golden rule of scholarships is: Unless a scholarship specifically says that you need to be a high school student to apply then you should feel free to apply for it as long as it matches your interests and goals. Remember, a college freshman can be 17 years old or 70 years old. It doesn't make a difference for these scholarships. Consider every scholarship that does not explicitly exclude you as fair game. Now let's roll up our sleeves and find some scholarships to win.

Looking For Scholarships In Your Community

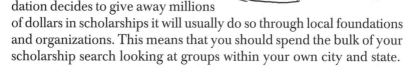

When you think about the errands you run around town, whether to the supermarket or library, you may not think of your community as a source of scholarship funds, but it is. Indeed, the very first place you should look for scholarships is in your own backyard. The majority of scholarship dollars are local dollars given by community groups, charities and foundations. Even when a large foundation decides to give away millions of dollars in scholarships it will usually do so through local foundations and organizations. This means that you should spend the bulk of your scholarship search looking at groups within your own city and state.

The downside of this approach is that there are few resources that list scholarships from these organizations since they are so local. This explains why many students ignore these scholarships. This brings us to the upside, which is that because they are harder to find, these scholarships will draw a lot less competition.

Begin your search in the following places in your community:

1.

Community service groups

Every city or town has various civic groups and public service organizations. Many of these groups spend the year fundraising to be able to award scholarships. While some may direct their awards through the local high school, you'll find others have awards open to future college students of any age.

There are also an increasing number of civic groups that are creating dedicated adult student scholarships. For example, the Chagrin Valley Junior Women's Club in Ohio offers a $1,000 scholarship to an adult female over the age of 25 who wants to return for an undergraduate education. Many local Rotary Clubs, which have long sponsored awards for high school seniors, are establishing similar awards for adult students. Since these scholarships are limited only to those who live in the community that the club serves, there are no national directories or lists of these scholarships. Even on the Internet there are no websites that offer a comprehensive list of local scholarships. Plus, new scholarships are constantly being created so any directory that you find is out of date from the first day it is published.

The best way to track down these awards is to check the Internet and make a list of the service clubs in your community. While you're at it, why not dial the number and ask if they offer a scholarship? Keep in mind that most service clubs also belong to a national organization. Both the local and the national organization may offer their own scholarships.

In addition to the Internet, visit your community center. The people who work there should know the names of most of the service clubs in your community. Your local public librarian can also help you track down these organizations.

To make sure you haven't missed any groups, get into your car and drive to the city limit. Usually on the same sign that welcomes visitors to your city is a modern day totem pole with the plaques of the various civic groups that are active in your community.

The following is a list of the larger service clubs with national affiliations. The websites provided are for the national organization. On the national website you should look both to see if they offer a scholarship and to find the contact information of your local chapters.

2. Altrusa

This international service organization proves that business is not all about the bottom line. Its members are business and professional leaders who are committed to community improvement through volunteerism.
Website: http://www.altrusa.com

3. American Legion

This community service organization has almost 3 million members who are all veterans. Almost every town in America has an American Legion post. With such a membership, you might expect that you'd need some connection to the military to win a scholarship. In truth what is most important is that you can demonstrate your contribution to your community. Military service is not required for most of their awards.
Website: http://www.legion.org

4. American Red Cross

Through its many local chapters the Red Cross provides a variety of services particularly during times of national disasters as well as related educational assistance.
Website: http://www.redcross.org

5. Association of Junior Leagues International

This women's organization is committed to promoting volunteerism, developing the potential of women and improving communities. Contact your local chapter to see what scholarships may be available.
Website: http://www.ajli.org

6. Civitan

Counting Thomas Edison as one of its members, Civitan is a volunteer organization that serves individual and community needs with an emphasis on helping people with developmental disabilities. On the national level ask about the *Shropshire Scholarship.*
Website: http://www.civitan.org

7. The Elks Club

The Elks Club is a fraternal organization dedicated to charitable works that has more than 2,100 Lodges and more than 1.1 million members. Many lodges have established their own scholarships for students in the community.
Website: http://www.elks.org

8. Fraternal Order of Eagles

Their slogan is "People Helping People." To make this a reality the Eagles build training centers around the world, raise money to combat heart disease and cancer and help both those with disabilities and seniors. Check your local club to see what scholarships they offer.
Website: http://www.foe.com

9. Kiwanis International

This is a worldwide club for service and community-minded individuals. Kiwanis perform all kinds of community-based service projects. Inquire with your local club about their scholarship opportunities for adult students.
Website: http://www.kiwanis.org

10. Knights of Columbus

The Knights of Columbus has become the largest lay organization in the Catholic Church and supports a variety of community and charitable programs. While the local councils establish their own scholarships, on the national level the *Father Michael J. McGivney Vocations Scholarship* and the *Bishop Thomas V. Daily Vocations Scholarship* are available to help students who are in theology programs.
Website: http://www.kofc.org

11. Lions Club International

The International Association of Lions is the largest service organization in the world with more than 1.4 million members. Lions members are dedicated to community service and other charitable goals. Almost all scholarships are awarded by local clubs.
Website: http://www.lionsclubs.org

12. The National Grange

Members of this organization share a common interest in community involvement and agricultural and rural issues. Check with your state Grange association for specific scholarships.
Website: http://www.nationalgrange.org

13. NeighborWorks

This is a national network dedicated to revitalizing neighborhoods through innovative local partnerships of residents, businesses and government. Contact your local NeighborWorks program to see if they offer a scholarship.
Website: http://www.nw.org

14. Performing arts center

You may think that your local performing arts center is just a place to watch singers and dancers. However, if you are a performer yourself, your local center may not only enhance you culturally but also financially. Often these non-profit organizations sponsor scholarship competitions in the arts. For a list of performing arts centers by state, visit http://www.performingarts.net.

15. Rotary Club
If you dream of living or working abroad, the Rotary Club can help fulfill your dream. This club brings together business and professional leaders to provide humanitarian service, encourage high ethical standards in all vocations and help build goodwill and peace in the world. On the national level find out about the *Ambassadorial Scholarships* and the *Cultural Ambassadorial Scholarships*. Many local clubs also sponsor scholarships in their communities. Ask specifically about any opportunities for adult or returning students.
Website: http://www.rotary.org

16. Ruritan
Don't think that you will miss out on scholarships just because you don't live in a major metropolitan area. Ruritan, a civic organization made up of local clubs in small towns and rural communities, offers several awards for local students. Ask your local club about the *Student Scholarship Program* and if they participate in the *Double Your Dollar Educational Grant Program*. Other educational grants are also available.
Website: http://www.ruritan.org

17. Salvation Army
The Salvation Army is dedicated to caring for the poor and feeding the hungry. It also sponsors and supports many youth programs. Check your local organization to see if they offer college scholarships.
Website: http://www.salvationarmyusa.org

18. Sertoma International
Their name stands for "SERvice TO MAnkind." This volunteer organization is dedicated to helping people with speech, hearing and language disorders. On the national level ask about the *Hearing Impaired Scholarships* and the *Communicative Disorders Scholarship Program*.
Website: http://www.sertoma.org

19. Soroptimist International of the Americas (SIA)
Your efforts may be rewarded with a scholarship if you're a young woman who volunteers, especially if your work benefits girls or women. Soroptimist members include women of all professions who believe in the importance of awareness, advocacy and action in the service of

community and society. On the national level ask about the *Woman's Opportunity Awards Program*. Check your local Venture Clubs of the Americas for other opportunities.
Website: http://www.soroptimist.org

20. U.S. Jaycees

The U.S. Junior Chamber (Jaycees) provides its members with an opportunity to develop as leaders in their communities by getting involved with civic affairs. On the national level ask about the *War Memorial Fund Scholarship*, *Thomas Wood Baldridge Scholarship* and *Charles R. Ford Scholarship*. Membership is not required for many of the awards.
Website: http://www.usjaycees.org

21. White House Office of Social Innovation and Civic Participation

This national effort to encourage volunteerism is coordinated at the White House. Its mission is to strengthen our culture of service and help find opportunities for every American to start volunteering. Look at the prizes and challenges under the office's initiatives.
Website: http://www.whitehouse.gov/administration/eop/sicp

22. Veterans of Foreign Wars

This advocacy group for veterans is also committed to promoting volunteerism and service. Your local VFW along with its Ladies Auxiliary may offer scholarships to students in the community.
Website: http://www.vfw.org

23. YMCA/YWCA

When you think of the YMCA, you might think of summer camp. But what you should think of is scholarships. With more than 2,400 branches, this organization provides a host of health and social services to the community. Contact your local Y to find out about local awards.
Website: http://www.ymca.net

24. Zonta International

This organization of business executives and professionals is dedicated to the improvement of the status of women worldwide. On the national level ask about the *Amelia Earhart Fellowship Fund* and the *Jane M. Klausman Women in Business Scholarship Fund*.
Website: http://www.zonta.org

What is the purpose of the scholarship essay?

There are two main reasons that you are asked to submit an essay with your scholarship application. The first is to show the scholarship judges why you deserve to win the scholarship. This does not mean that you should overtly campaign for your victory, composing a top 10 list of why you should be the winner, but you want to point out your achievements and be proud of your accomplishments. The second reason why you are asked to write an essay is to share something about yourself that is not conveyed in your application. Scholarship committees view essays as a way to learn more about you and to gain insight into who you really are. Don't just list off accomplishments that are also found in your application. Use your essay to help the scholarship judges get to know you better.

25.

Local charities and non-profit foundations

One of the growing sources of scholarship dollars is from local charities and non-profit foundations. These organizations often raise money for specific causes, and education is usually one of them. Many of the scholarships given by charities are aimed at students who otherwise could not afford to go back to school. Another common focus of these organizations is to help adults pay for training in specific vocational skills to help them re-enter the workforce or advance their careers.

For example, the Midland Area Foundation in Michigan (http://www.midlandfoundation.com) offers the *Dr. Shailer L. Bass Memorial Scholarship* for non-traditional students. This $2,000 award is for Midland County adults pursuing post-high school studies at a college or university.

Similarly the San Diego Foundation (http://www.sdfoundation.org) administers a variety of scholarships for its residents including the *Dorothy M. Bolyard Memorial Scholarship*, which is open to residents over the age of 24 who are pursuing a degree at a two- or four-year university in San Diego County. The foundation also offers the *Herman*

H. Derksen Scholarship, which is open to any resident who is pursuing a trade or vocational program. If you visit the website of the San Diego Foundation you'll find that the adult student scholarships are mixed in with the high school student scholarships. In fact, to apply for one of the adult scholarships you use the same application that high school students use for their awards. This underscores the importance of being thorough in your research and to not assume that just because a foundation sponsors a lot of scholarships for high school students that it doesn't also have some for adult students.

To find the charities and foundations in your area, visit your local public library and ask the reference librarian for a directory of local charities and foundations. Also, every time you speak to a charity to ask about scholarships make sure you also ask if they know of other groups that you can contact.

Here are a few Internet sites that provide a good list of charities in most areas. This is not a complete list so make sure you also do your own local research.

26. Charity Wire
On this site you can look for charities by type or cause. If you look under the "Miscellaneous" tab you'll find several scholarship funds. Website: http://www.charitywire.com

27. Community Foundation Locator
The Council on Foundations offers a nice clickable map on their website to help you find various foundations in your state. Website: http://www.cof.org/Locator/

28. Network For Good
This website lets you view charities by city and state. Use the menu at the top left of the page to find charities in your area. Website: http://www.networkforgood.org

29. Volunteer Match
This website helps to match people to volunteer opportunities. By typing in your zip code you can browse a list of openings

along with the name of the charity or non-profit organization.
Website: http://www.volunteermatch.org

30. Yahoo Directory

Yahoo lists a lot of charities. While somewhat cumbersome to use since it is not listed by state, this directory provides some good city resources. Starting with the top level, click on "Philanthropy," then "Community Service and Volunteerism" and then "Regional Information." Here you'll find links to such useful sites as "California Volunteer Sites" and the "Chicago Area Volunteer Opportunities." You should also explore the other subcategories in the Yahoo directory.
Website: http://dir.yahoo.com/Society_and_Culture/Issues_and_Causes/

31.

Churches and religious organizations

If you are a member of an organized religion ask your minister, pastor, reverend, rabbi, priest or monk if the church sponsors a scholarship. Many religious organizations offer awards to members of their congregation. If they don't, politely suggest that they should.

Make sure you also check out the national or international organization of the church since they may sponsor scholarships in addition to those offered by your local church. The following is a list of organized religions that offer national scholarships for their members.

32. Assemblies of God

On the national level the church offers a variety of scholarships including the *Touch With Hope Scholarship* for single mothers. The website also has a special section on college planning for Assemblies of God members at http://colleges.ag.org.
Website: http://www.ag.org

33. Baptist Church

The American Baptist Churches support American Baptist undergraduate, graduate and seminary students. To support growth in ministry skills, the church also assists pastors and those in other church voca-

tions. All applicants must be members of an American Baptist church for at least one year before applying.
Website: http://www.nationalministries.org

34. Catholic Church
The Catholic Aid Association provides educational support through the *College Tuition Scholarship*.
Website: http://www.catholicaid.com

If you are a member of the Catholic Workman Fraternal Benefit Society you may also qualify for their scholarship.
Website: http://www.catholicworkman.org

35. Church of Jesus Christ of Latter-Day Saints
If you plan to attend Brigham Young University, check out the website and visit the department in which you plan to major. Most have a list of scholarships available to students within the major and some are designated for Mormons.
Website: http://www.byu.edu

36. Evangelical Lutheran Church
Begin your search at the website of the Evangelical Lutheran Church in America. You can search the site for specific scholarships as well as find links to related organizations such as the Women of the Evangelical Lutheran Church in America. This group in particular offers a number of scholarships including the *Opportunity Scholarships for Lutheran Laywomen*.
Websites: http://www.elca.org

37. Judaism
There are a variety of scholarships for Jewish students. A good starting point is the Hillel: The Foundation for Jewish Campus Life, which sponsors several grant and scholarship competitions as well as produces several useful guides for Jewish students.
Website: http://www.hillel.org

Another useful resource is the Bureau of Jewish Education, which has branches in most major cities. You can use the telephone book or a search engine like Google or Yahoo to find the one nearest you. Once you locate a local Bureau, you'll notice that it often has a list of scholarships for local Jewish students. The website for the Bureau in

San Francisco, for example, has a page that lists most of the scholarships for Jewish students in Northern California.
Website: http://www.hillel.org

38. Methodist Church
The church sponsors several scholarship programs including the *Foundation Scholarship Program*, which awards $1,000 scholarships to more than 400 students. The church also has *Ethnic Minority Scholarships* and *General Scholarships* for older students and students who demonstrate leadership.
Website: http://www.umc.org

The General Commission on Archives and History also offers several research and writing grants for students interested in studying the history of the church.
Website: http://www.gcah.org

39. Presbyterian Church
The church offers a variety of awards to members who are enrolled in college. Graduate students may apply for the *Continuing Education Grant*, and medical students may apply for the *Grant Program for Medical Studies*.
Website: http://www.pcusa.org

40. Seventh-Day Adventist
Visit the church's website to find scholarship programs sponsored by individual churches.
Website: http://www.adventist.org

On the national level there is also the *General Conference Women's Ministries Scholarship Program*, which has awarded more than 550 scholarships since 1994. The scholarships are for women who plan to attend a Seventh-Day Adventist college and who otherwise would be unable to afford a Christian education.
Website: http://wm.gc.adventist.org

41. Society of Friends (Quakers)
The United Society of Friends Women International administers the *John Sarrin Scholarship*. This award provides money for students preparing for ministry.
Website: http://www.fum.org

How do I write a winning scholarship essay?

When it comes to actually winning a scholarship you need to write a powerful essay. Your essay is critical to convincing the judges to give you their money. When you are writing your scholarship essay, don't make any of the following mistakes:

Missing the question. It seems obvious, but enough students make this mistake that it needs to be emphasized: Be sure your essay answers the question.

Not having a point. If you cannot summarize the point of your essay in a single sentence, you may not have one.

Topic is too broad. Don't try to cover too much in the limited space of the essay.

Mechanical errors. Spelling and grammatical errors signal carelessness.

Not revealing something about you. Regardless of what the essay is about, it needs to reveal something about who you are, what motivates you or what is important to you.

Being ordinary. For your essay to stand out from the pile of other applicants, either the topic needs to be unique or the approach original.

If you want to learn more about writing a winning essay and read examples of successful scholarship essays, take a look at our book, *Adult Students: An Insider's Guide to Getting Into College.*

42. United Church of Christ

The church offers the *UCC Seminarian Scholarship* for students preparing for ministry. Certain colleges have also designated funds for students who are members of the United Church of Christ. Currently the colleges with special scholarships for UCC students include Catawba College, Cedar Crest College, Dillard University, Doane College, Drury University, Elmhurst College, Elon College, Heidelberg College, Hood College, Lakeland College, Olivet College, Pacific University, Ripon

College and Talladega College. You can check the national website for any additions to this list at http://www.ucc.org/scholarships/. In addition, the national offices of the United Church of Christ offer a limited number of awards from individual donors.
Website: http://www.ucc.org

43.

Your labor union

If you belong to a union or plan to enter a field that has one, be sure to check with the union for any potential scholarships. Many unions offer education benefits to their members. The American Federation of Labor-Congress of Industrial Organizations (AFL-CIO) maintains a directory of its member unions. The organization has also awarded more than $3 million through its Union Plus Scholarship Program. You can find more details at http://www.aflcio.org/About/Member-Benefits/Scholarships. If your union is not a part of the AFL-CIO, then go directly to your union representative and ask about their educational benefits.

44.

Local businesses—big and small

As a way to say "thank you" to customers, many businesses offer scholarships for students in their community. Take a look at all of the retail businesses, services and any corporate home offices that are in your area. The supermarket chain Fred Meyer, for example, offers scholarships through Portland State University to undergraduate students. In San Diego, Anheuser-Busch sponsors the *Eagle Achievement-Adult Scholarship* through the League of United Latin American Citizens.

To find businesses in your area, check with your local chamber of commerce. You can visit the national chamber of commerce online at http://www.uschamber.com and from there you can find your local chamber. Most chambers maintain a directory of member companies that you can view. Be sure to ask the people who work at the chamber if they are aware of any companies that award scholarships.

Whenever you are shopping, be on the lookout for awards. Many students have stumbled across scholarships by picking up a brochure at the cash register. If your city is the headquarters for any large company, investigate if that company offers a scholarship.

Most large companies offer scholarships through their own foundations. For example, Wal-Mart has the Sam Walton Foundation, while Bank of America has the Bank of America Foundation. These foundations are separate entities and you need to speak to someone who works for the foundation (not the company) to find out what specific scholarships may be available.

45.

Network with other adult students

You are not the first person to look for scholarships. In fact, dozens of adults in your area have gone through the same process of looking for scholarships. Why not make use of their knowledge? You can contact the admission office at colleges near you and ask to speak to a few adult students. You can also find people on the Internet who may be willing to share their knowledge. Of course, the most basic way to find people is to tell everyone you know that you are planning to go back to school and would love to speak to other adult students. When you meet with veteran adult students, ask them what resources they found helpful and what advice they have to make your search easier.

46.

Take money from your local politicians

Even if you didn't vote for them, you may get some help from your local politicians. Many establish scholarships for students who live in their district as way of saying "thank you" to their constituents. Contact your local politicians' offices to find out more.

47.

Search your community newspaper for past winners

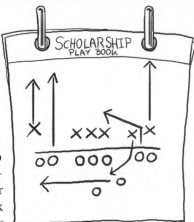

Your local newspaper is a treasure map to finding local scholarships. In the fall and spring local scholarship organizations announce their winners and your community newspaper prints their names. Go through back issues or search the newspaper articles online (search for the words "scholarship" and "scholarship winner") to find announcements of last year's scholarship winners. Even if the announcement is about a high school student winner, note which organization gave the award and inquire if there are others for adult students.

48.

State scholarships and grants

Every state offers grants to students. Look at Chapter 6 and contact your state's agency for higher education to learn about which grants you are eligible to receive. You'll find a variety of grants and scholarships along with a lot of helpful resources. Some state agencies will even do some of the work by providing you with a list of scholarship opportunities.

Don't Ignore Your College Or University

Whether you are still considering going back to college or are already in school, you should take advantage of all the resources that your college offers. Even if you are not yet in college you can still visit the school you're thinking of applying to and speak to people who can help.

Every college administers its own financial aid programs and has a certain number of scholarships that it awards to its own students.

Aren't all scholarships based on financial need?

The truth is that you could be the son or daughter of Donald Trump and still win a scholarship. There are basically two kinds of scholarships available.

As their name suggests, need-based scholarships are based on your financial need. To verify the level of your need, scholarship organizations may ask for tax returns or a copy of your Free Application for Federal Student Aid (FAFSA). Remember that the definition of need varies. Not all scholarships require extreme need. In fact, some organizations define families with incomes of up to $100,000 as needy. Also, it's important to know that need-based scholarships are not necessarily given to the most needy students. Many need-based scholarships also consider your academic and other achievements in addition to your financial situation.

On the other hand, merit-based scholarships do not take into account your financial status. Rather, they are based on other qualities such as your future plans, involvement in the community, talents or other achievements. For these kinds of awards, it doesn't matter how many digits are in your income. You win these scholarships by showing that your background and achievements make you the most deserving of the award.

One common misconception about college scholarships is that you must be a full-time student. The University of Minnesota College of Continuing Education, for example, offers both merit- and need-based scholarships for adult students who are enrolled full- or part-time. There are awards that cover a broad range of adult programs including non-admitted students enrolled in credit courses, degree and certificate students and students enrolled in non-credit continuing professional education and personal enrichment courses. The university has also developed eligibility requirements that are friendlier to adult students. Their need-based scholarships are based on current income rather than on previous tax year income, which is used for mainstream financial aid programs. This means that many more adults will qualify than they would under traditional guidelines. The university looks at other issues such as disability, previous access to education, time available for paid employment and the demands of juggling multiple roles of work and family when awarding scholarships. The university has a useful website for prospective adult students at: http://www.cce.umn.edu. While geared toward Minnesota residents, it still provides useful information to all adult learners.

While each college and university offers its own resources, here are some of the best places to start:

49.

The college financial aid office

If you are already in college (or even if you just live near one) pay a visit to the financial aid office. This office serves as a clearinghouse for scholarship opportunities at your school and within your community. Many financial aid offices maintain a list of scholarship opportunities. Even if you are not receiving financial aid you can still make an appointment to speak with a financial aid officer about the various scholarship opportunities at your college.

Almost all colleges also have a financial aid website. It's tempting to explore this website instead of actually visiting or calling the office. This can be a mistake. Financial aid offices are notoriously understaffed and overworked and updating their website may not be high on their list of priorities. So be sure to speak to a real person to ask specifically about scholarships.

50.

Adult education center or continuing education center

Many colleges now have an adult education or continuing education center. This may be a separate department or it may just be a specialist who works in the admission or financial aid office. Call or visit the office to ask what special services or resources they have for adult students.

51.

Career services office

Even before it's time to find a job with your newly minted degree, you can take advantage of your college's career services office. Most career services offices maintain lists of scholarships and in particular those that might help you get a summer internship or work during the term. Don't wait until your last year in college to see what the career services office has to offer.

52.

Department's administrative assistant

One of the most valuable people at your college is not the president of the school, the dean or even your favorite professor; it's the administrative assistant of your department. This one person knows more about what happens in your major than any other person. Take some time to talk to your department's administrative assistant. Ask him or her about what kind of scholarship opportunities and competitions are available to students with your major.

Here are just a few examples of what you might find. The University of Massachusetts at Amherst has such scholarships as the *Philip Weiss Memorial Scholarship* for students majoring in Judaic Studies, the *Butterworth Scholarship* for juniors and seniors studying floriculture or ornamental horticulture and the *Stephen R. Kellogg Scholarship* for sophomores in the civil and environmental engineering department. Just asking around within your own major will turn up a lot of possibilities.

53.

Campus clubs and organizations

It pays to be active. By joining clubs and getting involved with student organizations you will not only become a part of your college community but you will also be able to apply for scholarships. Many campus organizations and groups have scholarships for their members. By being active in these clubs, you have a chance of winning some of these awards.

54.

Ace your college applications to get more scholarships

You may not realize that your college applications are also scholarship applications. If the colleges really want you, then they will not only offer you admission but will also give you an automatic scholarship. Even if you know that you are a definite admission for the college you are applying to, spend the time and effort to create an outstanding application. That might be the difference between simply getting admitted and getting admitted with a $10,000 scholarship. If you want to learn more about how to ace your college admission applications, we recommend our book, *Adult Students: A Painless Guide to Going Back to College.*

55.

Don't let the colleges take away your scholarship money

When you win a scholarship, you have to report it to your college. Unfortunately, sometimes a college will decrease your financial aid by the amount of scholarship money that you win. Not fair, you say? You're absolutely right! If this happens to you, immediately contact the organization that gave you the scholarship and explain the situation. Some scholarship organizations have policies against giving an award to a student if the college will adjust their financial aid package. With the scholarship organization on your side, approach the college financial aid office. In most cases the financial aid office will back down rather than see you forfeit the scholarship.

If the college insists on adjusting your financial aid package, ask that they lower your student loan amounts rather than grants. It's much better for you to have to borrow less in loans anyway. Be firm in making your case and be sure to point out to the college that their policy gives you little incentive to apply for any scholarships in the future.

If none of these strategies work, you should still take the scholarship since it is guaranteed while any financial aid grants are subject to availability of the funds. Even if you get a grant in one year you might not receive the same amount the next year. But a scholarship, if it's renewable, will pay you the same amount every year.

Searching Beyond Your Community

You started your scholarship search by looking locally in your own community. You expanded it by exploring the resources that are offered by your college. Now it's time to explore the rest of the country to find scholarships.

56.

The Internet

The Internet puts the world's biggest library at your fingertips and allows you access to an unprecedented amount of information. It can also be truly frustrating. The problem with searching for scholarships online is that there is no filtering. Type in the word "scholarship" into a search engine and you'll get over 5,000,000 results. Only a tiny fraction of these results will actually be useful to you. To solve this problem of too much information there are specialized websites that let you search databases of scholarships. For the best of these, you fill out some information about yourself and with the click of a mouse are matched to scholarships that you may apply to win.

Sound too easy? In some ways it is. Don't rely on these websites to find every scholarship that's right for you. Many students make the mistake of assuming that once they do an Internet search they have exhausted all sources for scholarships. The reality is that no matter how many scholarships these websites claim to have in their database none of them even comes close to the total number of scholarships that are available. Plus, none of these websites does a good job of listing local scholarship opportunities–which as you've just seen offer you some of the best chances to get free cash for college.

Before we share our list of the best websites to search we want to warn you that these are all geared toward high school students. This means you'll get a lot of matches that you can't use. But that's okay. Even if you find just a single scholarship by performing a search, that is still one award that you may not have found on your own. We also want to warn you about any website that charges you money to perform a search. There are enough good free websites that you should never have to pay for a scholarship search. Your goal, after all, is to find money for college, not spend it on some dubious website.

57. SuperCollege
Website: http://www.supercollege.com

58. Sallie Mae
Website: http://www.salliemae.com/scholarships

59. MoolahSPOT
Website: http://www.moolahspot.com

60. Chegg
Website: http://www.chegg.com/scholarships

61. Mario Einaudi Center for International Studies
Although the site is for international students, many of the fellowships and scholarships listed are also open to non-international students.
Website: http://einaudi.cornell.edu/funding-opportunities/postdoc

62. The College Board
Website: http://www.collegeboard.com

63. Fastweb
Website: http://www.fastweb.com

64. The Princeton Review
Website: http://www.review.com

65. Scholarship Experts
Website: http://www.scholarshipexperts.com

66. Adventures In Education
Website: http://www.aie.org

67. FastAid
Website: http://www.fastaid.com

68. Scholarships.com
Website: http://www.scholarships.com

69. Petersons
Website: http://www.petersons.com

70. CollegeXpress
Website: http://www.collegexpress.com

71. CollegeNet
Website: http://www.collegenet.com

72.

Big business

When you think about how many cars Toyota and General Motors sell or about how many cans of Coca-Cola the world consumes, you can see why large companies like these might take some of their profits and return them to students through scholarships. Unfortunately, most of these big business scholarships are aimed at high school students. The exception is when companies use their scholarships to encourage students to enter a specific field, which is related to the company's focus. Tylenol, for example, offers $250,000 in scholarships for students of any age in health-related fields, which makes sense for a pharmaceutical company.

Think about what you are majoring in (or planning to major in) as well as what sort of job you hope to get after you graduate. Then think about all of the companies that make money from that profession. The best way to get your list started is to think of the industry that you are entering and then look at all of the companies within that industry.

For example, let's say that you are going back to school to finish up an English degree so you can work as an editor for a book publisher. So the "industry" that you want to enter is publishing, and if you look at the companies in this industry you'll find the likes of American Greetings Corporation, McGraw-Hill and even Martha Stewart Living Omnimedia. These are the companies that you'll want to explore more for scholarship opportunities since if they offer them, they will probably be for students who want to enter the publishing industry or who are majoring in areas such as English, journalism or writing.

Here are a few good resources to find both your industry and the their associated companies:

73. The New York Stock Exchange
This is the official website of the NYSE and it also lists all of the companies that are listed on the stock exchange. The website offers a fantastic breakdown of these companies by industry at https://www.nyse.com/network.
Website: http://www.nyse.com

74. The NASDAQ
We also have the NASDAQ stock exchange. From the homepage, look for the "Company List" page. From here you can view companies by industry. Unfortunately, the industry list is not as detailed as those of the AMEX and NYSE, which means that you will have to sift through a larger results page to find the right companies.
Website: http://www.nasdaq.com

75.

Professional associations

Whether you want to be a computer scientist or certified fraud examiner there is a professional organization to support your profession. In fact, in the U.S. alone there are more than 135,000 professional associations. One of the missions of these organizations is to support students who want to enter the field. Many of them accomplish this by offering scholarships.

In our scholarship book, *The Ultimate Scholarship Book*, we list many of the best professional organizations that offer scholarships. We recommend that you look at *The Ultimate Scholarship Book* as well as another book called the *Encyclopedia of Associations* published by the Gale Group. This is a multi-volume set that is extremely expensive to buy. Fortunately, you can find this book at most college libraries. Inside you will find a detailed list of nearly every association in the country.

Another way to find professional associations is to talk to the people who are already in these careers. If you're studying to be a dental assistant, spend some time talking to dental assistants and learn which associations they belong to. You can also go to the library and read the trade journals for the profession. Associations often advertise in these publications.

The following are just a few examples of the associations that offer scholarships. Remember, there are more than 135,000 of these kinds of associations out there and many offer scholarships.

76. Academy of Motion Picture Arts and Sciences
An Oscar may be in your future, so get a head start on the golden guy with these scholarships. Future filmmakers and screenwriters may apply for the *Don and Gee Nicholl Fellowships in Screenwriting* and the *Student Academy Awards*.
Website: http://www.oscars.org

77. Actors' Fund of America
It may be hard to make ends meet working as a waiter while waiting for your big break. That's why the *Actors' Work Program* provides tu-

ition and grants for job retraining for members of the entertainment industry.
Website: http://www.aflcio.org

78. Air Traffic Control Association
If your dream is to someday direct the traffic in the sky, you should check out the *Air Traffic Control Association Scholarship Program.*
Website: http://www.atca.org

79. Aircraft Electronics Association
This association offers a variety of awards for students interested in a career in avionics or aircraft repair. They administer the following awards: *Bendix/King Avionics Scholarship, Bud Glover Memorial Scholarship, David Arver Memorial Scholarship, Dutch and Ginger Arver Scholarship, Garmin Scholarship, Goodrich Aerospace Scholarship, Johnny Davis Memorial Scholarship, Lee Tarbox Memorial Scholarship, Lowell Gaylor Memorial Scholarship* and *Mid-Continent Instrument Scholarship.*
Website: http://www.aea.net

80. American Association of Airport Executives
If you love airports and could think of nothing better than spending 40 hours a week working in one then check out the *AAAE Foundation Scholarship.*
Website: http://www.aaae.org

81. American Association of Critical-Care Nurses
Active RN students and members of the AACN may apply for the *Educational Advancement Scholarship.*
Website: http://www.aacn.org

82. American Bar Association
Future lawyers can enter the *ABA Essay and Writing Competitions* or apply for the *Legal Opportunity Scholarship Fund.*
Website: http://www.abanet.org/lsd/

83. American Concrete Institute
There is no construction industry without cement. If you are a college senior interested in entering the construction industry, check out the *Peter D. Courtois Concrete Construction Scholarship.*
Website: http://www.aci-int.org

84. American Criminal Justice Association
Rewarding future crime fighters, the association offers both a scholarship program for undergraduate or graduate students who are studying criminal justice and a student paper competition for student members.
Website: http://www.acjalae.org

85. American Culinary Federation
Future chefs take note. If you are in a culinary program the *Chain des Rotisseurs Scholarship* and the *Chair's Scholarship* are available to exemplary students.
Website: http://www.acfchefs.org

86. American Dental Association
If you want to pursue a career in dental hygiene, dental assisting, dentistry or dental laboratory technology take a look at the *Allied Dental Health Scholarship*, *Dental Student Scholarship* and *Minority Dental Student Scholarship*.
Website: http://www.ada.org

87. American Institute of Chemical Engineers (AIChE)
If you're a member of an AIChE Student Chapter or Chemical Engineering Club you may apply for the *Donald F. and Mildred Topp Othmer Foundation Scholarship* or the *National Student Design Competition*. If you're not a member but are majoring in chemical engineering you may apply for the *John J. McKetta Scholarship*.
Website: http://www.aiche.org

88. American Meteorological Society
If you've ever dreamed of making it rain (or at least predicting when it will), look at these scholarships for atmospheric or oceanic studies: *AMS Undergraduate Scholarship*, *AMS Graduate Fellowship in the History of Science*, *Industry Minority Scholarship*, *Industry Undergraduate Scholarship*, *Industry/Government Scholarship* and the *Father James B. Macelwane Annual Awards in Meteorology*.
Website: http://www.ametsoc.org/AMS/

89. American Nuclear Society

If you are a student in a nuclear-related field, check out the *ANS Graduate Scholarship*, the *ANS Undergraduate Scholarship* and the *John Muriel Landis Scholarship*. The *Delayed Education Scholarship for Women* is available for adult, female students.
Website: http://www.ans.org

90. American Nursery and Landscape Association

If you have a green thumb then the *Timothy Bigelow and Palmer W. Bigelow, Jr. Scholarship* and *Usrey Family Scholarship* may be the perfect awards for you.
Website: http://www.americanhort.org

91. American Society of Agricultural and Biological Engineers

Biological or agricultural engineering majors are eligible for the *ASABE Foundation Scholarship*. The *Adams Scholarship* is available to scholars focusing on agricultural engineering.
Website: http://www.asabe.org

92. American Society of Ichthyologists and Herpetologists

If you are a future ichthyologist or herpetologist check out the *Gaige Fund Award*, the *Raney Fund Award* and the *Stoye and Storer Award*.
Website: http://www.asih.org

93. American Society of Mechanical Engineers (ASME)

ASME student members may apply to a number of scholarships including the *ASME Foundation Scholarship*, the *F.W. Beichley Scholarship*, the *Frank and Dorothy Miller ASME Auxiliary Scholarship*, the *Garland Duncan Scholarship*, the *John and Elsa Gracik Scholarship*, the *Kenneth Andrew Roe Scholarship*, the *Melvin R. Green Scholarship* and the *Robert F. Sammataro Pressure Vessel Piping Division Scholarship*. (If you understand what this last scholarship is about you probably deserve to win it!)
Website: http://www.asme.org

94. American Society of Travel Agents Foundation

We see travel in your future. If you do too then take a look at the various scholarship programs offered by this society, which include the *American Express Travel Scholarship*, the *Avis Scholarship*, the *Fernando R. Ayuso Award*, the *Healy Scholarship*, the *Holland America Line-Westours, Inc. Research Grant*, the *Joseph R. Stone Scholarship*, the *Princess Cruises and Princess Tours Scholarship*, the *Simmons Scholarship* and the *Southern California Chapter/Pleasant Hawaiian Holidays Scholarship*. The *A.J.*

Spielman Scholarship is specifically designed for re-entry students who are enrolled or scheduled to attend a recognized proprietary travel school.
Website: http://www.asta.org

95. American Society of Women Accountants Scholarship
Attention number crunchers. If you are a female part-time or full-time student of accounting, contact your local ASWA chapter to receive an application for the *ASWA Scholarship*. You do not have to be a member to apply.
Website: http://www.aswa.org

96. American Welding Society Foundation
If you are living your dream of working in the spark-filled welding industry then you'll want to apply for the *James A. Turner, Jr. Memorial Scholarship*.
Website: http://www.aws.org

97. Armed Forces Communications and Electronics Association
First of all you don't have to be affiliated with the military to apply for these scholarships. However, they are geared toward students in technical or scientific fields. Check out these awards: the *General John A. Wickham Scholarship*, *Ralph W. Shrader Scholarship* and the *Computer Graphic Design Scholarship*.
Website: http://www.afcea.org

98. Associated General Contractors of America
Planning on wearing a hard hat to work? If you are an undergraduate or graduate student in a construction or civil engineering program you may apply for the *AGC Undergraduate* or *AGC Graduate Scholarship*.
Website: http://www.agc.org

99. Associated Male Choruses of America
This association offers the *AMCA Music Scholarship* to promote chorus and music students in college.
Website: http://amcofa.org

100. Association for Women in Mathematics
To support women who are studying mathematics this organization sponsors both the *Alice T. Schafer Prize* and the *AWM Biographies Contest*.
Website: http://www.awm-math.org

101. Association for Women in Science

It's no secret that there are more men in the sciences than women. That's why the AWS sponsors the *Science Undergraduate Award* and the *Association for Women in Science Graduate Award* to encourage more women to pursue careers in the sciences. In particular, the *Ruth Satter Award* is designed for a graduate student who interrupted her education for at least three years to raise a family.
Website: http://www.awis.org

102. Association of Certified Fraud Examiners

If you want to make a career out of detecting forged checks, you may apply for the *Ritchie-Jennings Memorial Scholarship*, which supports students who want to become Certified Fraud Examiners.
Website: http://www.cfenet.com

103. Association of Food and Drug Officials

If your dream is to work for the FDA or if you are studying food, drug or consumer product safety, the Association of Food and Drug Officials offers scholarships to make your dream come true. The *George M. Burditt Scholarship* and *Betsy B. Woodward Scholarship* are available to students entering their junior and senior years.
Website: http://www.afdo.org

104. Association of State Dam Safety Officials

Somebody has to keep the dam from bursting. If that person is you, then don't ignore the *ASDSO Dam Safety Scholarship*.
Website: http://www.damsafety.org

105. Broadcast Education Association (BEA)

This is the award for future Peter Jennings and Katie Courics. If you are a college junior, senior or graduate student at a BEA member university you may be able to apply for the *Broadcast Education Association Scholarship*. The organization has members who are in the television and radio broadcasting industry as well as in telecommunications and electronic media.
Website: http://www.beaweb.org

106. DAR National Scholarship

The National Society of the Daughters of the American Revolution sponsors the *Enid Hall Griswold Memorial Scholarship,* which is awarded to both male and female students entering their junior or senior year of college who are majoring in political science, history or economics.

No affiliation with DAR is necessary. However, all applicants must obtain a letter of sponsorship from their local DAR chapter.
Website: http://www.dar.org

107. Educational Foundation for Women in Accounting
Do you like working with numbers? If so, the *Women in Transition Scholarship* and *Women in Need Scholarship* both provide financial assistance to female students who are pursuing degrees in accounting and are single parents or heads of households. Trying to get a Ph.D. in accounting? You may be interested in the *Laurel Fund.*
Website: http://www.efwa.org

108. Emergency Nurses Association
To promote research and education in emergency care this association sponsors a range of undergraduate, graduate and doctoral scholarships. Among these are the *ENA Foundation Undergraduate Scholarship,* the *Karen O'Neil Endowed Advanced Nursing Practice Scholarship* and the *Medtronic Physio-Control Advanced Nursing Practice Scholarship.*
Website: http://www.ena.org

109. Entomological Society of America
In combination with the Entomological Foundation (http://www.entfdn.org), the Entomological Society of America offers several scholarships. For undergraduate students, the *Stanley Beck Fellowship* and several other undergraduate scholarships are available. The *Stanley Beck Fellowship* is also available to graduate entomological students, as are the *John Henry Comstock Graduate Student Award* and the *Normand R. Dubois Memorial Scholarship.*
Website: http://www.entsoc.org

110. Executive Women International (EWI)
Single parents, individuals just entering the workforce or displaced workers may all apply for an *Adult Students in Scholastic Transition (ASIST) Award.*
Website: http://www.executivewomen.org

111. Golf Course Superintendents Association of America
Do you always find yourself defending golf's place in the sporting kingdom? If the golfing industry is your passion you have your pick of scholarships for every aspect of the golf course industry including: the *GCSAA Footsteps on the Green Award,* the *GCSAA Scholars Program,* the *GCSAA Student Essay Contest* and the *Scotts Company Scholars Program.*
Website: http://www.gcsaa.org

112. Herb Society of America

If you are passionate about studying herbs then you don't want to miss applying for a *HSA Research Grant*. Be sure to also check your local unit to see what scholarships they may offer.
Website: http://www.herbsociety. org

113. Industrial Designers Society of America

You may have the next winning design for robotic vacuum cleaners or 100 gigabyte mp3 players in you. Student industrial designers may apply for the *IDSA Undergraduate Scholarship*.
Website: http://www.idsa.org

114. International Association of Fire Fighters

Members of the IAFF may apply for the *Harvard University Trade Union Program Scholarship*. Selection is based on participation in your local IAFF affiliate. The *W.H. "Howie" McClennan Scholarship* is also available to the children, biological or adopted, of fire fighters who died in the line of duty.
Website: http://www.iaff.org

115. International Association of Plumbing and Mechanical Officials

As a part of the *International Water, Sanitation and Hygiene Foundation Essay Scholarship Contest*, students write an essay on clean water and sanitation systems.
Website: http://www.iapmo.org/Pages/EssayContest.aspx

116. International Food Service Executives Association

You probably know that there is more to food services than food preparation. The industry needs students who are skilled in management. If you are studying a food service-related major then check out the *IFSEA Scholarship*.
Website: http://www.ifsea.com

117. International Society for Optical Engineering
Undergraduate or graduate students studying optics, photonics, imaging, optoelectronics or a related field may apply for the *SPIE Educational Scholarship*. For students specifically studying optical design there is the *Kidger Scholarship*.
Website: http://www.spie.org and http://www.kidger.com.

118. Iron and Steel Technology
To attract talented and dedicated students to careers within the iron and steel industries, this organization offers the *Willy Korf Memorial Fund Scholarships*, the *Ronald E. Lincoln Memorial Scholarship* and the *Benjamin F. Fairless Scholarship* to full-time students with majors in metallurgy, metallurgical engineering or materials science.
Website: http://www.aistfoundation.org

119. Karla Scherer Foundation Scholarship
The Karla Scherer Foundation has traditionally supported students who are studying finance and economics. However, recently the foundation has changed its focus and is now aimed solely at helping women entering the master's of arts program in the humanities at the University of Chicago.
Website: http://www.karlascherer.org

120. National Association of Broadcasters
For the *Freedom of Speech PSA Contest*, students create a 30-second TV or radio public service announcement about freedom of speech.
Website: http://www.nabef.org/freedomofspeechpsa/default.asp

121. National Association of Chiefs of Police
The *NACOP Scholarship* is for severely disabled officers who want to retrain through education. It is also open to the college-bound children of disabled officers.
Website: http://www.aphf.org

122. National Association of Corrosion Engineers
The *NACE Foundation Academic Scholarship* assists students who are pursuing science and engineering degrees.
Website: http://www.nace-foundation.org

123. National Association of Women in Construction
Don't think that only the guys get to have the fun with building things. If you are a female student enrolled in a construction-related degree

program you may apply for the *Undergraduate Scholarship*. Women engaged in a construction-related training program may apply for the *Construction Crafts Scholarship*.
Website: http://www.nawic.org

124. National Community Pharmacists Association
Students who are enrolled in a college of pharmacy may apply for the *NCPA Foundation Presidential Scholarship* or the *J.C. and Rheba Cobb Memorial Scholarship*, each of which is worth $2,000.
Website: http://www.ncpanet.org

125. National Press Photographers Foundation
If you are studying photojournalism or want to enter this industry, take at look at the following awards: the *Bob East Scholarship*, the *College Photographer of the Year Award*, the *Joseph Ehrenreich Scholarship*, the *Kit C. King Graduate Scholarship*, the *NPPF Still Photography Scholarship*, the *NPPF Television News Scholarship* and the *Reid Blackburn Scholarship*.
Website: http://www.nppa.org

126. National Restaurant Association Educational Foundation
Students majoring in a food service/hospitality or restaurant-related program may apply for the *Academic Scholarship for Undergraduate College Students*.
Website: http://www.nraef.org

127. National Society of Accountants
The *NSA Scholarship* is perfect if you're an undergraduate majoring in accounting with a minimum 3.0 GPA.
Website: http://www.nsacct.org

128. National Society of Professional Engineers
This association offers a variety of scholarships for future engineers. The *Professional Engineers in Industry Scholarship* and the *Paul H. Robbins, P.E., Honorary Scholarship* are available to undergraduate students. Graduate students may apply for the *Professional Engineers in Government Scholarship* and the *Professional Engineers in Industry Scholarship*.
Website: http://www.nspe.org

129. National Speakers Association
Surveys show that people fear speaking in public more than death. If you're an exception, the *Bill Gove Scholarship*, the *Cavett Robert Schol-*

arship, the *Nido Qubein Scholarship* and the *Earl Nightengale Scholarship* are for you.
Website: http://www.nsaspeaker.org

130. National Student Nurses' Association
Students in an approved school of nursing or pre-nursing program may apply for the *National Student Nurses' Association Scholarship*.
Website: http://www.nsna.org

131. Outdoor Writers Association of America
If writing, filming or creating art based on the great outdoors is what you love, you might have a chance at the *Bodie McDowell Scholarship*.
Website: http://www.owaa.org

132. Physician Assistant Foundation
American Academy of Physician Assistants members who attend an accredited physician assistant program may apply for the *Physician Assistant Foundation Scholarship*.
Website: http://www.aapa.org

133. Plumbing-Heating-Cooling Contractors National Association
If you are currently in a p-h-c program (and if you are then you know this means plumbing-heating-cooling), then you may be able to apply for the *Delta Faucet Company Scholarship*, the *PHCC Educational Foundation Need-based Scholarship* or the *PHCC Educational Foundation Scholarship*.
Website: http://www.phccweb.org

134. Public Relations Student Society of America
Publicity hounds and members of the PRSSA may apply for the following scholarships: the *Gary Yoshimura Scholarship*, the *Professor Sidney Gross Memorial Award*, the *Betsy Plank/PRSSA Scholarship*, the *Multicultural Affairs Scholarship*, the *Stephen D. Pisinski Memorial Scholarship* and the *Lawrence G. Foster Award for Excellence in Public Relations*.
Website: http://www.prssa.org

135. Radio and Television News Directors Association
If you plan to enter the fast-paced world of television or radio news broadcasting then you may want to take a look at the Radio and Television News Directors Association's many scholarships. For undergraduates, the *Carole Simpson Scholarship*, the *Ed Bradley Scholar-*

ship, the *Ken Kashiwahara Scholarship*, the *Lou and Carole Prato Sports Reporting Scholarship*, the *Mike Reynolds Scholarship*, the *George Foreman Tribute to Lyndon B. Johnson Scholarship* and the *Presidents' Scholarship* are all options. Graduate students may apply for the *Abe Schechter Graduate Scholarship*.
Website: http://www.rtnda.org

136. Society of American Registered Architects
If you're a budding architect, you can participate in this group's *Student Design Awards Program*.
Website: http://www.sara-national.org

137. Society of Automotive Engineers
Who knew that fixing up cars and trucks would lead you to a scholarship? This organization offers awards for college and graduate students entering this industry including the *Long-Term Member Sponsored Scholarship*, the *Ralph K. Hillquist Honorary SAE Scholarship* and the *Yanmar/SAE Scholarship*.
Website: http://www.sae.org

138. Society of Exploration Geophysicists
To encourage students who want to journey to the center of the Earth (or at least pursue a career in exploration geophysics), this association offers the *SEG Scholarship*.
Website: http://www.seg.org

139. Society of Nuclear Medicine
Students in nuclear medicine may apply for the *Paul Cole Scholarship Award*.
Website: http://www.snmerf.org

140. Society of Plastics Engineers
If you plan to enter the plastics industry then you are in luck. This organization offers a plethora of awards for future plastic people including the *American Plastics Council (APC)/SPE Plastics Environmental Division Scholarship*, the *Composites Division/Harold Giles Scholarship*, the *Polymer Modifiers and Additives Division Scholarship*, the *SPE General Scholarship*, the *Ted Neward Scholarship*, the *Thermoforming Division Memorial Scholarship*, the *Thermoset Division/James I. MacKenzie Memorial Scholarship* and (our favorite) the *Vinyl Plastics Division Scholarship*.
Website: http://www.4spe.org

141. Society of Professional Journalists

This group sponsors the *Mark of Excellence Awards* honoring the best in student journalism. There are awards in 45 categories for print, radio, television and online journalism.
Website: http://www.spj.org/ifs.asp

142. University Aviation Association

This association offers several awards for aviation students including the *Eugene S. Kropf Scholarship*, the *Gary Kiteley Executive Director Scholarship*, the *Joseph Frasca Excellence in Aviation Scholarship*, the *Serving Others Scholarship* and the *Paul A. Whelan Aviation and Aerospace Scholarship*. Scholarships from affiliated organizations may also be found at the website.
Website: http://www.imis100us1.com/UAA

143. Wilson Ornithological Society

Helping young students everywhere in their avian (bird) education and research, this society offers the *George A. Hall and Harold F. Mayfield Award*, the *Louis Agassiz Fuertes Award* and the *Paul A. Stewart Award*.
Website: http://www.wilsonsociety.org

How do I describe my accomplishments to impress the scholarship judges?

Winning a scholarship is about impressing the judges and showing them why you are the best candidate. Your accomplishments, activities, talents and awards all help to prove that you are the best fit. Since you will probably list your work experience and activities on the application form, you can use your essay to expand on one or two of the most important. Don't just parrot back what is on your application. Use the opportunity to focus on a specific accomplishment; provide detail and context. Listing on your application that you were a stage manager for a play does not explain that you also had to design and build all of the sets in a week. The essay allows you to expand on an achievement to demonstrate its significance.

144.

Don't ignore scholarship books

Even though they lack the pizzazz of the Internet, scholarship books should not be overlooked. A good book provides a huge number of awards and an index to help you find the ones that match your achievements and background. There are a lot of scholarship books—and most are somewhat expensive—so we recommend that you head to your local library or counseling center and browse through their collection.

One that we recommend, and it is not an impartial opinion by any means, is our book, *The Ultimate Scholarship Book.* We wrote this book after getting frustrated with many traditional scholarship books that cost too much and gave too little. We wanted to write a book that listed awards that most students could win. We also wanted to make sure that we didn't just give you the scholarships to apply to but that we also showed you how to win. In *The Ultimate Scholarship Book* you'll find that the first half of the book is a detailed strategy guide on how to create a winning scholarship application. The second half of the book is a comprehensive scholarship directory of hundreds of awards that you may apply to win.

Complementing our scholarship directory is our other scholarship book, *How to Write a Winning Scholarship Essay.* In this book you can read the essays of 30 scholarship winners and get tips directly from the scholarship judges who decide whether or not you win.

Regardless of whether you read our books, you should not ignore the value of traditional scholarship books and directories. They are a great source of awards as well as tips on how to win.

145.

Scholarships for a disability

Many organizations that work on behalf of specific physical or mental disabilities offer scholarship programs. Contact them directly or visit their websites to see what scholarships are available. The Easter Seal Society, for example, offers scholarships through local chapters for students with disabilities. Contact your local Easter Seal Rehabilitation Center to see what scholarships are available in your area. The same is true of most of the other organizations. Here are a few to get you started.

For the hearing impaired:

146. Alexander Graham Bell Association
The Alexander Graham Bell Association for the Deaf and Hard of Hearing is both the world's largest and oldest membership organization to promote the use of spoken language among deaf and hearing-impaired adults and children. This association offers its *College Scholarship Awards* to full-time students who are deaf or hard of hearing.
Website: http://www.agbell.org

147. National Fraternal Society of the Deaf
The National Fraternal Society of the Deaf is a life insurance/social service organization run by and for the deaf or hard of hearing. They offer $1,000 scholarships to members who are already enrolled in or are entering their post-secondary education.
Website: http://www.nfsd.com

148. Travelers Protective Association
The Travelers Protective Association is dedicated to community work in travel safety, child safety and other community service initiatives. They have established the *TPA Scholarship Trust for the Deaf and Near Deaf* to provide financial aid to people who are deaf or hearing impaired.
Website: http://www.tpahq.org

For the visually impaired:

149. American Foundation for the Blind
The American Foundation for the Blind is devoted to eliminating the barriers that might prevent those who are blind or visually impaired from reaching their full potential. Scholarship opportunities for both undergraduate and graduate students are available with the *Delta Gamma Memorial Scholarship*, the *Ferdinand*

Torres Scholarship, the *Karen D. Carsel Memorial Scholarship*, the *R.L. Gillette Scholarship* and the *Rudolph Dillman Memorial Scholarship*.
Website: http://www.afb.org

150. Association for Education and Rehabilitation of the Blind and Visually Impaired

The Association for Education and Rehabilitation of the Blind and Visually Impaired is an international association dedicated to giving aid to those who have devoted their lives to educating and rehabilitating the blind and visually impaired. This association offers the *William and Dorothy Ferrell Scholarship* to legally blind students who plan to pursue employment in the area of support services for the blind and visually impaired.
Website: http://www.aerbvi.org

151. Christian Record Services

The Christian Record Services provide free Christian publications and programs for the blind and visually impaired. The *CRS Scholarship* is available to people who are designated as legally blind.
Website: http://www.christianrecord.org

152. National Federation of Music Clubs

The National Federation of Music Clubs is a non-profit organization dedicated to music education and promotion of the performing and creative arts. It offers a wide range of scholarships to those majoring in various music-related fields. The *NFMC Gretchen E. Van Roy Music Education Scholarship*, the *NFMC Ruth B. Robertson Music Therapy Award* and the *NFMC Marion Richter American Music Composition Award* are just a few of the many scholarships this association offers.
Website: http://www.nfmc-music.org

153. National Federation of the Blind

The National Federation of the Blind operates with the intent of helping blind people achieve self-confidence and to act as a vehicle for self-expression for the blind. Thirty scholarships are available to legally blind post-secondary students of all levels, ranging from freshmen to doctoral candidates.
Website: http://www.nfb.org

How do I actually win a scholarship?

To win a scholarship you should follow these five tips. You can learn more in our scholarship book, Get Free Cash for College.

Be accurate and complete. More applications are disqualified because applicants didn't follow the directions than for any other reason.

Uncover the mission of the scholarship. Understand what the organization is trying to achieve by giving the scholarship and demonstrate how you match their goal.

Don't write your scholarship essay the night before. Give yourself time to write an essay that shows the judges exactly why you are the best candidate for their award by highlighting an experience or achievement that demonstrates how you match the goals of the scholarship.

Ace the interview. Interviews are often where final decisions are made, so be prepared by practicing your answers.

Don't be afraid to brag. This is not the time to be modest. Throughout your scholarship essay and interview explain why you deserve to win.

For physical disabilities:

154. Bank of America
One of the scholarships provided by Bank of America, the *Bank of America ADA Abilities Scholarship Program*, provides financial aid to legally disabled post-secondary students who intend to pursue a career in banking. Applicants must be under the age of 40 and be studying the fields of finance, business or computer systems.
Website: http://www.scholarshipprograms.org

155. Microsoft Scholarships for Students with Disabilities
Microsoft's award is aimed at current college students who are interested in entering the software industry.

Website: http://careers.microsoft.com/careers/en/us/intern-ships-scholarships.aspx

156. Pfizer
Pfizer offers the *Pfizer Epilepsy Scholarship* to college students with epilepsy.
Website: http://www.epilepsy-scholarship.com

157. Spina Bifida Association of America
The Spina Bifida Association of America has established the *SBAA Scholarship Fund* to provide financial aid to students with spina bifida. One-year scholarships are available to students of all ages.
Website: http://www.sbaa.org

For learning disabilities:

158. International Dyslexia Association
The International Dyslexia Association is dedicated to the study and treatment of dyslexia. Check your local association for scholarship opportunities.
Website: http://www.interdys.org

159. The Pat Buckley Moss Society
The Pat Buckley Moss Society is a membership organization formed with the goals of assisting charities and fostering an appreciation of the art of Pat Moss. The *Judith Carey Memorial Scholarship* is available to undergraduate or graduate students pursuing a degree in special education.
Website: http://www.mosssociety.org

Scholarships Just for Adult Students

Scholarships Just For Adult Students

One of the most common questions we are asked is, "Are there scholarships specifically for adult students?" The answer as you will see from this chapter is, "Absolutely!" There are many scholarships that are just for adult students.

In this chapter we will highlight some of the larger scholarships that are aimed at adult students. In compiling this list we wanted to make sure that they were open to adults across the country and could be used at almost any college. While we know this list will give you some good places to start applying, please keep in mind that new scholarships are established every day. It's important that you continue to do your own detective work and view these awards as just the beginning.

Note that many awards for adult students come from local organizations, which means that you should search all of the places we described in the previous chapter. It's also important that you never stop looking for scholarships. Continue looking and applying for scholarships throughout your entire time in school.

We will conclude this chapter with a list of scholarship contests. While these contests are open to all students, they also welcome students of every age. So if you are feeling lucky you might want to enter a few of these contests in between filling out applications for the other scholarships.

Ardella's Story

Even if you have never met Ardella Hudson, it's hard not to cheer for her and be impressed by her accomplishments. Ardella returned to school to work toward a bachelor's degree in social work at the College of St. Catherine in St. Paul, Minnesota.

Ardella readily describes herself as a 48-year-old product of social welfare. "I belong to four generations of the struggles of African American women to free themselves from welfare and poverty. The process of change often occurs in small increments over an extended period of time. It requires patience, but the payoff is great," says Ardella.

The impetus to going back to school was both sudden and traumatic. Ardella was an equipment operator when she suffered a debilitating injury on the job. As she recovered in the hospital she began to re-evaluate her life and realized that her job was simply not giving her the intellectual stimulation that she craved. Ardella also realized that since her son was grown and had a family of his own, she was no longer a single parent who was the head of a household. Free of her parental responsibilities, Ardella felt she could finally do something for herself. For the first time in her life she had the opportunity to fulfill her dreams. "I knew that if I loved what I did for a living it would not feel like work," she says.

Ardella's first major obstacle was an old student loan that had not been paid. "In the beginning I was told I could not get financial aid until all my old loans were repaid," she recalls. But Ardella was not one to give up so easily. She persisted in making inquiries with the financial aid office until she finally got in touch with the assistant director. He told her to pay $35 a month for six months and then call back so her account could be re-evaluated.

In the meantime Ardella had already started classes and was only able to pay for her first semester through a generous personal loan from a friend and by convincing the college to allow her to carry a balance on her account. After six months of making payments on her old student loans and regular visits to the financial aid office, she was finally able to work out a deal that allowed her to be considered for financial aid. It also didn't hurt that during that time Ardella had made the Dean's List every semester.

Since getting financial aid was so difficult, Ardella quickly turned to private scholarships. She found a scholarship offered by the Minneapolis Women's Rotary, which was aimed at women over 30 who wanted to change their lives. To apply Ardella had to write an essay describing why she wanted to earn a degree and what she planned to do with it. She won the $1,500 scholarship. While the money was a huge help, she also found that there was another benefit.

"This scholarship turned out to be worth more than money since I am able to attend all the monthly meetings and eat dinner with this group of women. This has turned out to be a wonderful experience for me," she says.

Ardella's second scholarship was from the Jeannette Rankin Foundation, a group that is dedicated to helping women over the age of 35 who want to better themselves through education.

From her experience, Ardella encourages other adult students, advising them to not let money hold you back from getting a college education. She suggests that you go to the school, speak to the financial aid office, apply for all the scholarships that you can and explain your desire to your family, letting them know that there may be some hard times ahead but it will be worth it because of what it will do for you.

Ardella also has this warning for adult students, "Do not have too much pride to ask for help. Such pride will only get you into trouble. You wouldn't be going to school if you knew everything. The whole process is a learning experience."

Despite the challenges she has faced, Ardella believes that everything she has gone through, the challenges, the experiences and the responsibilities, have all been worth it. "Before making the decision to go back to school I asked myself this question: 'Was I, a woman, who was part of the fourth generation of poverty in my family, worth the challenges, experiences and responsibilities that school could bring me?' The answer to my question was a definite 'yes.' It continues every day to be 'yes.' And I want to let all other non-traditional students know that each of you are worth it too."

Scholarships For Adult Students

160. A. Harry Passow Classroom Teacher Scholarship
This award sponsored by the National Association for Gifted Children is given to NAGC members who wish to continue their education. You must be a teacher of gifted students of grades K-12.
Website: http://www.nagc.org

161. Adult Students In Scholastic Transition (ASIST)
Executive Women International offers this award to assist adults who face major life transitions. Applicants may be single parents, individuals just entering the workforce or displaced workers.
Website: http://www.executivewomen.org

162. American Business Women's Association
This organization is dedicated to the support of women's professional development and career advancement in the business world. As a member of this organization you may be able to take advantage of specific grants for approved career development classes and programs.
Website: http://www.abwa.org

163. American Legion Auxiliary
The sister organization of the American Legion is the American Legion Auxiliary. This group places a high value on community service and offers an award just for adult students, the *Non-Traditional Student Scholarship.*
Website: http://www.legion-aux.org

164. Assistance League
Branches of this national organization give scholarships for adult students. For example, the Assistance League of Phoenix provides a scholarship for women and men who have completed 64 hours of community college and plan to earn a degree from a four-year college.
Website: http://www.assistanceleague.org

165. ASL Adult Education Foundation Scholarship
Each year the national chapter of Alpha Sigma Lambda Honor Society awards eight scholarships to adult student members. Scholarship applications are sent to all national councilors in early spring, and you should check with your chapter.
Website: http://www.alphasigmalambda.org

166. Association on American Indian Affairs Scholarship Programs

This organization has several scholarship programs that help Native American students pay for their higher education. All of the scholarships require the applicant be at least 1/4 degree Indian blood and from a federally recognized tribe. Awards include: *Emergency Aid and Health Professions Scholarship, Sequoyah Graduate Fellowship, AAIA/Adoph Van Pelt Special Fund for Indian Scholarship, AAIA/Florence Young Memorial Scholarship, AAIA/Norman M. Crooks Memorial Scholarship* and the *Displaced Homemaker Scholarship.*
Website: http://www.indian-affairs.org

167. Business and Professional Women's Foundation Career Advancement Scholarship

Sponsored by the BPW Foundation, this award helps disadvantaged women who want to further their education. Each year the foundation awards over $120,000 to women over the age of 25.
Website: http://bpwfoundation.org

168. Career Development Grants For Women

The American Association of University Women offers financial support for women who hold a bachelor's degree and are preparing to advance their careers, change careers or re-enter the work force. The AAUW also offers academic grants, which help women pay for master's degrees, second bachelor's degrees or specialized training. For example, the *Selected Professions Fellowships* are awarded to women who intend to pursue a full-time course of study in designated degree programs where women's participation traditionally has been low.
Website: http://www.aauw.org/fga/

169. Career Transition for Dancers

The award from the *Actors' Fund of America/Actor's Work Program* is for dancers who are seeking second careers. You must be over 27 and have 100 weeks or more of paid employment earned within AEA, AFTRA, AGMA, SAG or AGVA within seven years or longer.
Website: http://www.careertransition.org

170. Chips Quinn Scholarships

If you are a Chips Quinn alumnus you may apply for a scholarship to attend journalism and newsroom-management seminars. You must have been working at least three years in newspaper newsrooms and

have the endorsement of your current newspaper's editor to apply.
Website: http://www.chipsquinn.org

171. Continuing Education Awards
The Medical Library Association helps MLA members develop their
knowledge of librarianship through continuing-education programs.
You must already hold a graduate degree in library science and be a
practicing health science librarian.
Website: http://www.mlanet.org/p/cm/ld/fid=43

172. Continuing Education Grant/Loan Program
This program aids Presbyterian Church (U.S.A.) members pursuing
postgraduate educations. Applicants must be PCUSA church members
enrolled in a Ph.D. or postgraduate program in religious studies.
Website: http://www.pcusa.org/financialaid/scholarships.htm

173. Educational Foundation for Women in Accounting
The *Women in Transition Scholarship* and *Women in Need Scholarship*
both provide financial assistance to female students who are pursuing
degrees in accounting. Trying to get a Ph.D. in accounting? You might
just be interested in the *Laurel Fund.*
Website: http://www.efwa.org

174. Eleanor Roosevelt Teacher Fellowships
The American Association of University Women provides professional development grants for women
public school teachers, especially in
math, science and technology.
Website: http://www.aauw.org/fga/

175. Elizabeth Greenshields Foundation Grants
This award promotes an appreci-
ation of painting, drawing, sculp-
ture and the graphic arts through
supporting art students, artists or
sculptors. To apply you must have
already started or completed training at an established school of art
or have demonstrated through past
work and future plans that you will

make art a lifetime career.
Website: http://www.elizabethgreenshieldsfoundation.org

176. Evalee C. Schwarz Charitable Trust for Education

This trust provides interest-free loans to undergraduate and graduate students who demonstrate exceptional academic performance and significant financial need. Applicants must qualify for need-based government grants, which are awarded through the federal financial aid program.
Website: http://www.evaleeschwarztrust.org

177. First Data Western Union Foundation Scholarship Program

This program is designed specifically for non-traditional students who have overcome personal challenges, exemplify initiative, exhibit a commitment to learning and working hard and demonstrate financial need. Special consideration is given to applicants who show academic promise and a strong desire for advancing their educational and career goals.
Website: http://foundation.westernunion.com

178. Frank G. Brewer Civil Air Patrol Memorial Aerospace Award

This award is for applicants who have made noteworthy aerospace achievements over a number of years.
Website: http://ae.capmembers.com

179. Golden Key GEICO Adult Scholar Awards

If you are a member of the Golden Key Society and are an adult student you may apply for this award. You must have already completed at least 12 undergraduate credit hours in the previous year before you apply.
Website: http://www.goldenkey.org

180. Herb Gardner Foundation Award

The *AAMI Foundation / TISCOR (Herb Gardner Foundation) Award* recognizes mid-career biomedical professionals who seek to advance their careers by pursuing an undergraduate or advanced degree or completing training at a technical school.
Website: http://www.aami.org/awards/

181. Jeannette Rankin Foundation

This foundation raises money to help women who want to better themselves through education. You may apply for an award if you are over

35 and plan to pursue an undergraduate or vocational education.
Website: http://www.rankinfoundation.org

182. Kazimour Scholarship
Members of the Association for Non-Traditional Students in Higher
Education may apply for this program, which includes three $500
awards, two for undergraduate students (two-year and four-year) and
one for a graduate student.
Website: http://www.antshe.org

183. National League of American Pen Women
Founded in 1897 as an alternative to the all-male National Press Club,
this organization is for women journalists, authors and illustrators. The
organization offers the *Mature Woman's Scholarship Fund* to aid and
encourage professional development.
Website: http://www.americanpenwomen.org

184. Rita Levine Memorial Scholarship
Sponsored by the MENSA Education and Research Foundation, this
essay-based award is for women who are returning to school after
having had to interrupt their educations.
Website: http://www.mensafoundation.org

185. Society of Women Engineers (SWE)
This organization offers *National SWE Scholarships* for students from
freshmen in college through graduate and adult students. Re-entry
scholarships are also available for women in engineering who wish
to reenter the workforce after a period of absence.
Website: http://www.societyofwomenengineers.org

186. Tylenol Scholarship
Paging future doctors and nurses. You can win one of ten $10,000 or
one of 150 $1,000 scholarships from Tylenol if you are an undergradu-
ate or graduate school student who has demonstrated leadership in
community and school activities and who intends to enter a health-
related field.
Website: http://www.tylenol.com/news/scholarship

187. USA Funds Access to Education Scholarships
This need-based scholarship program is open to individuals who
plan to enroll or are enrolled in full- or half-time undergraduate or

graduate coursework. Winners are chosen based on their academic performance, leadership, activities, work experience and career and educational goals.
Website: http://www.usafunds.org

188. Wal-Mart Associate Scholarship
This scholarship is awarded to students who have been employed by Wal-Mart Stores for at least six months. You may receive up to $3,000 for part-time or full-time enrollment.
Website: http://www.walmartfoundation.org

189. Western Union Foundation Scholarship Program
This program is designed specifically for non-traditional students who have overcome personal challenges, exemplify initiative, exhibit a commitment to learning and working hard, and demonstrate financial need. Special consideration is given to applicants who show academic promise and a strong desire for advancing their educational and career goals.
Website: https://foundation.westernunion.com/education_programs. html

190. Women's Opportunity Awards
Sponsored by Soroptimist International, this award helps women who are heads of their households and are entering or re-entering the workforce to obtain education and skills training. Applicants must also be attending or have been accepted to a vocational/skills training program or an undergraduate program. Apply first at the community level through your local Soroptimist club.
Website: http://www.soroptimist.org

191. Women's Philanthropic Education Organization Grants and Scholarships
The P.E.O. has awarded more than $59 million in educational loans, $12 million in grants for continuing education and $2 million in scholar awards. The *P.E.O. Educational Loan Fund (ELF)* is a revolving loan fund established to lend money to female students for higher education. The *P.E.O. Program for Continuing Education (PCE)* provides need-based grants to women whose education has been interrupted and who find it necessary to return to school to support themselves or their families. *The P.E.O. Scholar Awards (PSA)* were established to provide substantial awards to women who are pursuing advanced degrees or are engaged in advanced study and research at an accredited institution.
Website: http://www.peointernational.org

Scholarship Drawings

Some people are born lucky. If you consider yourself lucky or just feel lucky you might want to enter a few contests that are only open to students. All of these contests are easy to enter and can be done over the Internet. The major drawback is that your fate is totally beyond your control.

192. eCampusTours $1,000 Scholarship Drawing
You can win one of ten $1,000 scholarships by registering.
Website: http://www.ecampustours.com

193. GoCollege Lucky Draw
Each month this website gives away prizes, including a first prize of a $250 scholarship.
Website: http://www.gocollege.com

194. NextStep Magazine
Winners are randomly selected for a $1,500 scholarship.
Website: http://www.nextstepmagazine.com

195. Scholarship Detective Scholarship
Winners receive a $1,500 scholarship.
Website: http://www.scholarshipdetective.com/scholarship

196. SuperCollege Scholarship Drawing
Sign up to win this college scholarship awarded through a random drawing.
Website: http://www.supercollege.com

197. Sallie Mae $1,000 Scholarship Drawing
Each month Sallie Mae selects a registered user to receive a $1,000 scholarship. Registration is free and you also get access to some cool resources such as a free scholarship search.
Website: http://www.salliemae.com

Maximize Your Federal Financial Aid

Getting Your Share Of Federal Financial Aid

Each year more than $238 billion is awarded in financial aid. It's an almost inconceivable amount. With this much money being paid out you definitely need to make sure that you get every penny that you deserve.

The biggest mistake that most adults make is not applying for financial aid because they assume that they won't qualify. Regardless of your income don't assume that you won't get any financial aid. The reality is you'll never know what you truly deserve unless you apply. You may find that even if you don't get a grant, you are awarded a cushy campus job, special college scholarships or low-interest student loans. One of these sources may be just what you need to make paying for college possible.

Here's a chart from a recent U.S. Department of Education study. It is not surprising that as income rises the percentage of students who received financial aid decreases. But even for families that earned over $100,000 per year, more than 71 percent of them still received financial aid.

Family income	Percent of students who received financial aid
Below $20,000	95.6 percent
$20,000-40,000	90.6 percent
$40,000-60,000	90.7 percent
$60,000-80,000	80.3 percent
$80,000-100,000	76.7 percent
Above $100,000	71.6 percent

These statistics underscore the danger of second guessing the financial aid office. Applying for financial aid is free and only costs you a few hours of your time. The rewards (remember that $238 billion) can be well worth the effort.

Jane And Marilou's Story

Jane Rabanal and Marilou Woolm both decided to return to graduate school, Jane at the age of 33 and Marilou at 50. While almost a generation apart, both women had similar reasons for returning to school.

For Jane, it was an unfulfilled feeling in the pit of her stomach, which began to nag at her. "I was unfulfilled at my work at the time and had come to know what I really wanted to pursue," she says. While Jane's undergraduate degree was in architecture, her work experience showed that her true passion was product design. To make a successful career switch, Jane quit her job and enrolled in a graduate program in industrial arts/product design at San Francisco State University.

Having worked for 10 years in a professional environment, deciding to go back to school was not easy. "It was a hard decision," Jane explains. "I felt comfortable at my job and that I was leaving a potentially successful path. Having been in the professional environment for years created a fear of leaving that behind."

Marilou also felt that she needed to change careers, but the turning point came after having major surgery. This experience made her realize that it was time for her to take action and do something that she had always dreamed of doing. She left a lifelong career in real estate management to go back to the University of Nevada in Reno to earn her master's degree in social work.

Once the decision was made, both women began to look for ways to pay for their educations. As Jane began to investigate her financial aid options she found that the only thing she would qualify for were unsubsidized loans. She says she didn't initially qualify because she had a substantial income prior to going back to school.

With her challenge made clear, Jane set out to find a way to receive a tangible financial aid package that would allow her to return to her graduate studies. "Financial aid does not account for the immediate income loss—it's a complicated transition to make," she reflects. Her first decision was to start aggressively saving money. Even now her savings is partially responsible for getting her through school. She saved over $10,000 before making the transition and worked part-time for about a year so that she would be eligible for financial aid. Eventually Jane received grants based on both need and merit. She also discovered there were scholarships available and received a *Graduate Equity Fellowship*, which is based on students' socio-economic upbringing, whether their parents attended college and other factors.

While Jane was trying to qualify for financial aid, Marilou was meeting with an academic counselor at the local university to figure out how she was going to pay for her degree. Marilou says her overall financial aid experience was a good one. "It actually made it possible for me to return to school," she explains. However, it was quite hard for her to take care of her two daughters and still make ends meet. Marilou ended up borrowing the maximum amount in student loans allowed from the Department of Education, obtained a Pell Grant and received grant money from private organizations.

Marilou feels the most difficult thing for her when returning to school was the process—but she was ready for it. "Due to my age, I was used to dealing with the system. For the young it would have been extremely frustrating," she says. Marilou has been working as a graduate assistant 20 hours a week and was also elected president of a graduate student organization, a paid position.

Both women are well on their way to earning their degrees. When she completes her master's, Jane intends to work in design consulting and eventually establish her own firm. "I love the kind of work that I am doing in school," she underscores. "I am really driven towards creating the kind of professional opportunity I seek once I graduate."

Marilou would like to stay at the university and work at a counseling center. "I did some price comparisons prior to starting graduate school," she explains, adding, "A master's degree pays twice as much. I look at it as an investment in myself." Marilou also knows that there is a high demand for social workers in Nevada and soon she'll be one of those highly sought after professionals.

Getting Started With Financial Aid

The financial aid process begins with providing detailed information on your personal finances through a form known as the Free Application for Federal Student Aid, or FAFSA. Using your prior-prior year's (PPY) taxes you will reveal all of the money that you have in savings, investments and hidden Swiss bank accounts. If you are applying to a private college you may also have to provide additional information through the college's own financial aid form or the College Board's CSS/Financial Aid PROFILE form. Like the FAFSA, it asks similar questions about your finances.

You can download a copy of these forms and even complete them online at http://www.fafsa.ed.gov for the FAFSA and http://www.collegeboard.com for the PROFILE.

You can turn in the FAFSA as soon as possible after October 1. Turn in your applications as early as possible since each college has its own deadlines, which are usually in early to mid-February. Plus, most colleges award financial aid until they run out of money. This somewhat first-come, first-served process means that the earlier you turn in your forms the better.

You will submit your FAFSA to the government for processing. The government will in turn pass on the results of their calculations to you in the form of the Student Aid Report (SAR) as well as to each college that you are applying to. It is important to understand that all the government does is crunch the numbers you provide on the FAFSA and pass the results to the colleges. This means that you need to indicate on the FAFSA which colleges should receive the results.

We want to point out that you are filling out your financial aid forms nearly seven months before you start school and using tax returns that

---

What is the timeline for applying for financial aid?

September-December
Focus on your college admission applications.

October-February
Complete and submit your financial aid applications.

March
Review your Student Aid Report, which will be sent to you after you submit your FAFSA.

April
You should receive both your college acceptance letters and financial aid packages. Review and compare your aid packages. Ask for a reassessment, if necessary.

May
This is the typical deadline for accepting all or part of your financial aid package.

---

will be two years old. This is an important point to keep in mind since anything that happens to your finances now won't affect your financial aid situation. In other words, your financial aid package for the 2018-2019 school year is really based on the 2016 tax year. Everything that happens to you financially after December 31, 2016, won't even be seen by the colleges when it comes to your financial aid forms.

With a detailed picture of your financial situation, each college financial aid office will analyze the money you have and figure out your degree of financial need based on the cost of the college. Once they know how much you need, they put together a financial aid package, spelling out how much and in which form you will get this money.

How To Determine Your Financial Need

To understand how the college determines if you have financial need you need to understand what the college does with all of the information that you provide.

198.

Know the difference between the Institutional and Federal methodologies

Public and private colleges have adopted different formulas and procedures for determining how much money you can afford to pay for college. Public schools (and some private ones too) use what is known as the Federal methodology. This is the formula provided by the U.S. Department of Education. When you submit the Free Application for Federal Student Aid (FAFSA), the government uses the information you provide to calculate the amount of money that you can put toward college for one year. The Federal methodology looks at things like your income and assets but does not consider assets such as retirement accounts and equity that you have built up in your home.

Some private colleges want to know about your retirement accounts and home equity as well and will use what is known as the Institutional methodology. By completing the College Board's PROFILE form in addition to the FAFSA, you will give the colleges some additional financial information. While the Institutional methodology is somewhat stricter than the Federal methodology and will usually result in less financial need, you really don't have a choice in the matter since you need to submit the financial aid applications the colleges require.

The goal of both the Federal and Institutional methodologies is to take the numbers you provide on the FAFSA and PROFILE forms, run a series of calculations and end up with a single number. This number is known as your Expected Family Contribution (EFC).

199.

Get to know your Expected Family Contribution

The Expected Family Contribution is the magic number. It represents the amount of money that you are expected to contribute for one year of your education. This number can range from $0 to infinity.

About two weeks after you submit the FAFSA you will receive the Student Aid Report (SAR), which will indicate your Expected Family

Contribution. You might want to sit down before you view the SAR. For the PROFILE you will not be told your Expected Family Contribution, but you can guess that it will be somewhat higher than the number on your Student Aid Report.

It's important to understand that the Expected Family Contribution is calculated by simply feeding the numbers you provide into a computer. Every person's data is run through the same calculation. Two different people with identical numbers on their FAFSA will have the same Expected Family Contributions. There are no special circumstances or explanations needed at this stage, and it won't do you any good to send a letter along with your FAFSA describing how tough it is for you to make ends meet. Save that letter for the next step. At this point you are just providing accurate information on your finances based on your tax returns.

But the game is not over yet. Once your Expected Family Contribution has been determined, it is passed on to the colleges you have applied to or the college you attend and is used to determine if you have financial need. It is at the college level where the exact composition of your financial aid package is determined. And, it is at this point that the computers are turned off and human beings take over.

200.

How your magic number–a.k.a. your Expected Family Contribution–is determined

At this point you are probably wondering how in the heck the government uses a snapshot of your finances to determine how much you can spend on college. Like everything from taxes to Social Security benefits, to calculate your Expected Family Contribution, the government uses a formula.

In general the formula, which can change from year to year, takes a percentage of your income and a percentage of your assets to calculate how much you have to pay for college. For example, the formula might assess up to 47 percent of your gross adjusted income (plus adjustments) and 5.65 percent of your total assets as being available to pay for tuition. The specific percentages are calculated based on family size and number of students in your family in college at the same time. There are also income and asset protection figures that prevent the government from touching everything that you have.

The easiest way to get an estimate of your Expected Family Contribution is to use an online EFC calculator. The Department of Education offers a free one at http://studentaid.ed.gov/fafsa/estimate. You can use it to get a quick estimate of your EFC. You can also change the numbers to simulate various changes in your finances. If you are a paper person you can also do all of the calculations by downloading an EFC worksheet at http://www.ifap.ed.gov. Click on the heading "Worksheet, Schedules and Tables."

For now let's keep things simple. The biggest factor in determining your Expected Family Contribution is your income. While your assets may be larger, they are not assessed at nearly the same level as your income. For example, for a hypothetical 34-year-old student who is not married, has no children, earns $40,000 in adjusted gross income and has $10,000 in savings, the Expected Family Contribution is about $13,363. (Remember, this is a hypothetical case and the numbers are approximations. Your specific situation even if you have the same income and assets may be different since the allocation of your income and assets are different.) Now if we were to assume that this student's income increases by $10,000 so that now she is earning $50,000 a year in adjusted gross income, her Expected Family Contribution would jump to about $17,216. However, if we assume that instead of having $10,000 more in income this student had $10,000 more in savings (i.e. assets) her Expected Family Contribution would be $15,363. The same $10,000 makes a big difference depending on whether it is in the form of income from a paycheck or cash in the bank. When the money is in the form of income, this student's EFC rises by $3,800. But when the same amount is in the form of cash in the bank, the student's EFC only increases by $2,000.

Right away you can see that changes in your income will affect your Expected Family Contribution more than changes in your assets. If you can lower or shelter your income (and to a lesser extent your assets) you can effectively lower your Expected Family Contribution.

What Counts As Expenses

Before we look at how to lower your Expected Family Contribution, we need to point out just a few details about what counts as income and assets. When you pay your taxes you don't get taxed on everything that you make. You make deductions and shelter some of your money from the tax collector. The same is true when calculating your Expected Family Contribution. Let's take a quick look at what are legitimate debts that will reduce your income or assets in the eyes of financial aid.

201. Your family expense sheet does not count as debt

Debt has always been a touchy subject. Colleges are very strict about what they consider debt that can reduce your income. They will not subsidize a family's expensive habits. If a family makes $8,000 a month in income but has expenses of $7,500 a month for such things as car payments, gardener bills, annual family trips to Europe, dinners at the finest restaurants, payments for the big screen TV, etc. then that's too bad. All of these discretionary expenses are not used to reduce your income. Be careful how you think about your income, and don't assume that your family expenses will be taken out when figuring out your income. Colleges consider your adjusted gross income that you report on your taxes to be your annual income.

202. Credit card debt is not debt when it comes to financial aid

If you need one more reason not to carry credit card debt (besides the outrageous interest rate), consider the fact that any credit card balances and interest paid will not lower your income for the purposes of financial aid. In reality these debts certainly take money from your pockets. Many families with high consumer debt are surprised at how much money colleges think they can afford. Remember that these debts are considered discretionary and often reflect a family's living style rather than a necessity.

203. Car payments will not lower your income

Car payments will not lower your income for financial aid. Therefore, the lower your payments the better. If you have a choice, pick a less-expensive car and avoid financing.

204. Mortgage payments will not lower your income

Under both the Federal and Institutional methodologies your home mortgage or home equity loan payments will not reduce your income.

Where do I get the FAFSA?

You can get your Free Application for Federal Student Aid by visiting http://www.fafsa.ed.gov or by calling 800-4-FED-AID. Most public libraries and financial aid offices also have FAFSA forms available.

The same is true for a passbook loan. However, unlike credit card interest payments you can deduct your mortgage or home equity loan payments from your taxes.

205. Your savings and checking accounts are assets

Under both the Federal and Institutional methodologies anything in your savings or checking accounts are counted as assets that you can use to pay for college. Fortunately, compared to income these assets are assessed at a much lower rate. There is no legal way to hide these assets.

206. Your stock and bond portfolios are assets

Under both the Federal and Institutional methodologies any stocks or bonds that you hold, which are not in retirement accounts, are fair game for the colleges to assess as available to pay for college. You should not radically alter your investment strategy or holdings just to get a few extra bucks from financial aid. It is just not worth the trouble, and you'll probably lose more than you'll gain.

207. Retirement accounts cannot be touched

Under most circumstances money in retirement accounts will not be counted as an asset and therefore cannot be touched by the colleges. Stocks, bonds and mutual funds held in normal accounts, even if you intend to use them for retirement, will be counted as an asset. To shelter your retirement money, you need to have it in an IRA or 401k type of account.

208. Your house may or may not be an asset

Under the Federal methodology your home is not considered an asset. However, under the Institutional methodology a portion of your home's value may be considered an asset. This presents an interesting option. If you move money from your savings account, for example, into your home by adding a new roof you are effectively sheltering your assets from at least the Federal methodology and possibly also the Institutional methodology for calculating your Expected Family Contribution. But, and this is a big downside, you are spending money that you might need to pay for college. Remember there is no guarantee that the college will be able to fund your entire financial need even if you have a low Expected Family Contribution. Also, as you will see, financial aid may come in the form of a loan, which may cost you more than if you had just used your savings.

However, consider the case where you have a leaky roof that needs to be replaced and it's more than two years before you start college. If you replace your roof now, as opposed to a year from now, you will reduce your savings account and therefore make yourself more eligible for a higher financial aid package. If you wait two years then it will be too late since you will already be in college. (Remember, financial aid is always based on the prior-prior tax year so anything you do to reduce your income or assets must be done more than two years before you apply for financial aid.) Of course, all of this assumes that you don't need the roof money to pay for living necessities. If you desperately need the money for something else, then it would be better to just live with a bucket in the living room.

Lower Your Expected Family Contribution

Now that you understand what counts and doesn't count as income or assets, you can use this information to try to lower your Expected Family Contribution. It's very important to remember that the following are generalized strategies that may not be appropriate for your individual situation. These are not hard and fast rules since what might be good for one family may be terrible for another. Before taking any action, speak with your accountant to make sure that the strategy will work for your individual financial situation.

209. Keep yourself poor

Every dollar in your name that is not in a retirement account is fair game for the college. Now in most cases you can't control how much money you have. It certainly is not worth volunteering to take a pay cut just to get a few extra dollars in financial aid! You simply would not get enough in financial aid to make up for the loss of income. However, there may be situations where you have some flexibility. For example, let's say that your parents decide that they want to start gifting money to you as part of their estate planning. As soon as that gift money hits your accounts (even if it is in the form of stocks or bonds) it becomes an asset that the college can assess against. If you know that you are going back to school you might want to ask them to hold off gifting you that money until you are in your last year of college.

210. Consider sheltering your money with your children

It might be tempting to consider giving some of your money to your children in the form of custodial accounts or 529 savings plans. While there are some good tax reasons for doing this, keep in mind that this money will eventually affect your children when it's their turn to apply for financial aid. However, the effect is minimal, and if you were planning on opening a custodial account or 529 savings plan anyway then it certainly wouldn't hurt if you do it before you apply for financial aid.

211. Consider deferring bonuses and raises

Imagine this scenario. It's November 2017 and you will be starting college in the fall of 2019. Your boss tells you that you will get a bonus or significant raise. If you take the bonus now, then that money will be used when determining your financial aid package for the 2019-2020 school year. Remember financial aid is always based on the prior-prior tax year. If you delay taking your bonus for two months until January 2018, then that money will not be used in your financial aid calculations for your first year. It will be counted when you apply for financial aid for the second year of college. But since you will have spent some (maybe even a significant amount) to pay for the first year and may have even stopped working to go to school, you will have less assets and income anyway. Under this scenario, taking the bonus in 2018 would not affect your financial aid package as much as if you had taken the bonus in 2017.

Before you consider this, be sure that you are going to get financial aid in the first place. Also consider other factors such as will your boss still be in the mood to give you a bonus next year? Sometimes it's better to just take the money.

212. Consider alternative forms of bonuses

If you have the flexibility, it may make sense to take your bonus or even a pay raise in some other form than cash. Of course, if you need the money then take the cash, but if you are in a situation where there is an equally useful alternative then you might want to consider it.

For example, instead of taking a raise you might swap one day a week of working from home, which could save you money in other ways such as lower childcare costs. Or you might convert your bonus from a cash payment to having your company pay for training or classes that you were planning to pay for yourself. A bonus or raise that does not show up as income will not be subjected to financial aid consideration. However, carefully weigh the costs of forgoing a cash bonus or pay raise. If you can use the money to pay down credit card debt, for example, you are probably much better off doing that.

213. Time your stock sales

When you sell a stock or redeem a bond can have an impact on your financial aid. Let's say you have a stock that has appreciated. You plan to start college in August 2019. If you sell the stock any time after January 1, 2017, the earnings are considered income and will be assessed by the college. But let's say that instead you sell the stock before January 1, 2017 (in other words at least two years before you start school). Now the gain will not be counted as income but instead show up as an asset in the form of more money in your savings account. As an asset this money will be assessed at a lower percentage than if it were income.

214. Build your 401k or IRA accounts

Under both the Federal and Institutional methodologies your retirement accounts are not considered assets that can be used to pay for college. Plus, under current tax laws you can withdraw money from these accounts and use them to pay for college without paying a penalty. So don't neglect your retirement as you save for college.

215. Buy essential school supplies before you submit your financial aid forms

The strict accounting definition of "assets" is the value of everything that you own. However, for financial aid "assets" are only the value of the cash and investments that you own at the time you complete the financial aid form. This means that things like computers, cars and clothes are not considered assets for financial aid. If you know you are going to need a laptop computer once you start school, consider buying it before you complete the financial aid forms. This way you are converting the assets in your bank account, which can be assessed as available to pay for tuition by the college, into assets (i.e. a laptop computer) that cannot be assessed to pay for tuition.

Now don't go crazy and run off on a shopping spree. This strategy works only because you were planning on buying the computer anyway. You are simply purchasing the computer now, before you submit the financial aid forms, instead of later. But by doing this you are lowering your assets in the eyes of financial aid.

Some students have taken the above tactic to the extreme and blown all of their money on something foolish like a new Jaguar convertible. While you could do so and deplete your savings account in the process, the extra money you gain in financial aid (which may be in the form of a student loan) will not even come close to the money you spent. Plus, with your savings depleted you have no safety net to make up for the gap between financial aid and what your college actually costs. Remember, your savings is your most valuable resource and you should not waste it frivolously on the off chance that you might get additional financial aid.

216. Take a year off of work before going to school

It may sound extreme but some adults decide to take a year off of work before applying to school. They may drop down to part-time instead of full-time which effectively reduces their income. After a year of lower income they apply for financial aid and qualify for a higher amount. While this strategy might sound tempting there are some major considerations. First, you need money to live during that year without work. Also, remember that you would need to do this two years before starting school. If you can't survive on your part-time salary or if you must dig into your savings to live, it is simply not worth it. You also need to figure out how much you would be able to save if you continued to work full-time until you entered college. If that amount is more than the amount you could receive from financial aid then you should stick with work since your salary is a sure thing while financial aid is not guaranteed for everyone.

Yet, despite these risks it is a fact that some adults have used this strategy successfully to pay for school. Be sure you weigh all of the benefits and risks before you make this decision. Also speak to a financial aid officer at your college to see what kind of package you could expect (and how much of that would be composed of student loans) so you can make an informed decision.

217.

There is a human being behind all financial aid decisions

Up until this point financial aid looks very analytical. It seems like you just plug in the numbers and out pops your Expected Family Contribution. But the story of financial aid does not end with your Expected Family Contribution. After your EFC is computed, the rest becomes a very human process. Your EFC will be sent to every college you are applying to, and this is where the computations end and human beings take over.

At the colleges, financial aid officers use your EFC as a guide when putting together your aid package. The financial aid officer has the ability to raise or lower your EFC for a variety of reasons. Therefore, it is crucial that you are open about your family's true financial situation to the financial aid officer. Remember too that all financial aid is based on your prior-prior year's taxes. A lot may have happened this year that is not reflected by the prior-prior year's taxes. If you want to share additional information, you can send a letter to the college financial aid office to explain any unusual circumstances that may affect your family's finances. Most colleges actually include a space on their financial aid forms for you to describe any relevant information. When you are thinking about writing this letter, consider the following three points.

218. Don't hide the dirty laundry

Most people when filling out financial forms feel compelled to hide embarrassing circumstances. After all you are revealing your financial strengths and weaknesses to a total stranger. However, if you have extraordinary circumstances such as large medical bills, unemployment, recent or ongoing divorce, extended family members to support or any additional expenses that may not be reflected in your FAFSA or PROFILE, tell the financial aid officer. Don't be embarrassed. It could cost you big time.

219. Give the college a reason to give you more money

Financial aid officers are numbers people. However, they have wide latitude for interpreting numbers and may apply a variety of standards and make exceptions, which can help or hurt your case. To get the most support from these professionals, make your case with numbers. You can't just say that you don't have enough money. You need to show it. Document with numbers why your tax forms don't accurately reflect your true income or expenses.

220. Don't try to trick the college

The human being in the financial aid process is also what keeps it safe from trickery. You could, for example, take all of the money in your savings account and plunk it down to buy an around-the-world vacation. On paper you have no savings. Yet, when the financial aid officer looks at your income, he or she will think it is very odd that someone who earns a decent living and owns a nice house is so cash poor. This is a red flag, and you'll be asked to provide additional information. Once the financial aid officer learns how you spent your savings, not only would he or she not give you more financial aid but you would also have no money left to pay for college even if you wanted to.

Financial aid officers are experts at reading financial statements. Just by looking at your 1099 interest statements they can get an estimate of the size of your assets. Trying to trick the college or not report certain income or assets will only backfire. Financial aid officers are professionals who have seen every trick in the book. Our best advice on trickery is to not attempt it.

221.

How to determine your financial need

Once you know your Expected Family Contribution, it's easy to determine your financial need. All you do is take the total cost of attending a specific college including tuition, room and board, books and travel expenses and subtract it from your Expected Family Contribution.

The difference is your financial need. It's important to remember that individual schools, not you, determine the total cost of attendance.

Let's look at an example and assume that your college costs $9,000 per year for tuition. Add the average expenses for books and miscellaneous expenses and the total cost of attendance may be $18,000 per year. You have submitted both the FAFSA and PROFILE forms. This means that the college has received your Expected Family Contribution as determined by the Federal and Institutional methodologies. For argument's sake let's assume that under the Federal methodology your Expected Family Contribution is $5,000 and under the Institutional methodology it is $6,000. (Remember the Institutional methodology is usually stricter.) If the school only uses the Federal methodology it will take the $18,000 for the total cost of attendance and subtract the $5,000 that your family is expected to contribute. That leaves your family with a financial need of $13,000. If the school is a private college that uses the Institutional methodology, your financial need is $12,000.

It is this amount, your financial need, which the school must now figure out a way for you to afford. They can give you money in the form of grants, student loans and work-study. Or, it is possible that the school won't be able to find all of the money, leaving you with what is known as "unmet need." The exact composition of your financial aid package will depend on a variety of factors and will vary by college.

222.

How your financial aid is packaged makes a difference

Let's assume that your Expected Family Contribution is lower than the cost of one year in college and therefore you have financial need. Once that amount is determined it is up to the financial aid office at the college to try to put together a package that will meet that need. The college may not always be able to do it and unless it is the college's policy to meet all financial need of its students, then the college is under no obligation to provide anything. Of course, most colleges will try.

The way in which your aid is packaged will differ not only because your financial need changes with the price of each college but also because colleges have varying amounts of financial aid resources.

When should I apply for financial aid?

Apply for financial aid as soon as possible after October 1. Don't wait until after you are accepted by a college to apply. If you do the college may have already allocated all of its money. When it comes to financial aid the early bird does get the worm.

The following is a detailed description of what you might find in your aid package. Most financial aid packages consist of a combination of these sources.

223. Federal Pell Grants

These grants are for undergraduate study for students who have the most financial need. The amount varies based on your EFC, but the current maximum amount is $5,815. All students who apply for financial aid by completing the FAFSA and are determined to have financial need by their college will be considered for Federal Pell Grants.

224. Federal Supplemental Educational Opportunity Grants

These grants are for undergraduates with the most financial need. The government provides limited funds for individual schools to administer this program. This means there is no guarantee that every eligible student will receive an FSEOG Grant. The amount varies between $100 and $4,000 per year, and the specific amount is determined by the college on a case-by-case basis.

225. Grants from the college

The college itself has various need- and merit-based grants. By applying for financial aid you will be considered for these grants. Some schools also have grants reserved just for adult students.

226. State grants

Your state may offer both need- and merit-based grants. While some grants are administered by the state, others are distributed to the colleges to administer.

227. Federal Work-Study

Work-study provides jobs for undergraduate and graduate students with financial need allowing you to earn money while attending school. The focus is on providing work experience in your area of study. Generally, you will work for your school on campus or for a non-profit organization or public agency if you work off campus. You will have a limit on the hours you can work in this program. Your wages are based on the federal minimum wage although they are usually higher.

228. State Work-Study

Besides the federal program, some states also have a work-study program that mirrors the operation of the federal program.

229. Federal Perkins Loans

Federal Perkins Loans are low-interest loans for undergraduate and graduate students with extreme financial need. Your school provides the loan from governmental as well as its own funds. You can borrow up to $5,500 per year as an undergraduate or $8,000 per year as a graduate student. The interest rate is fixed at 5 percent and there are no additional fees.

230. Subsidized and Unsubsidized Federal Direct Loans

Through the William D. Ford Federal Direct Loan program, you may borrow up to $9,500 as an independent freshman, $10,500 as a sophomore and $12,500 as a junior or senior undergraduate student or up to $20,500 per year if you are a graduate student.

Depending on your financial need you may be offered a subsidized or unsubsidized Direct loan. When the loan is subsidized the government pays for the interest that accrues while you are in college and before you start to repay it. For unsubsidized loans you must pay the interest that accrues while you are in college although you don't start making any payments until after you graduate from college. You need to demonstrate financial need to receive a subsidized loan but not for an unsubsidized loan. For more detailed information about student loans, see Chapter 5.

231.

You can pick and choose from your financial aid offer

When you receive an offer of financial aid you don't have to accept or reject the whole package. You are free to pick and choose the specific pieces of aid you want. If you are offered a grant you'll definitely want to accept it, but you might not want to accept the loan component. When you are analyzing your award package consider each piece separately.

232.

Get into the right mindset

When you're sitting in front of the computer, you may have a feeling of dread at the thought of filling out the FAFSA. Tell yourself that it usually takes about 30 to 60 minutes to complete the form. When you think about it, that's a small investment of time for the possible reward!

233.

Colleges run out of money so turn in applications early

The deadlines for turning in your financial aid applications vary by college. You want to turn in your FAFSA as soon as possible after October 1. The reason is that colleges have a limited amount of financial aid. If you turn in your application late, even if you deserve aid you may not get it simply because the college ran out of money.

234.

Think about financial aid early–at least two years before you start school

Remember that all of the numbers used in financial calculations come from the prior-prior tax year. If you are starting college in September

2019, then your tax return from 2017 will be the basis for that first year. Therefore, if you wait until January 2017 to think about financial aid it will be too late to do anything that will affect the outcome of your first year. (Of course, you could still do things to affect your financial aid for your second year in school.)

235.

You must apply for financial aid every year

Financial aid is determined on a year-by-year basis. That means that even if you didn't get financial aid this year you should apply next year since your finances will have changed, especially after paying for one year of tuition. Some students find that after the first or second year of college they have reduced their income and assets to the point where they qualify for financial aid. There is a Renewal FAFSA that you can use, which saves a lot of time when applying for aid the next year.

236.

Use your financial aid application as an insurance policy

Nobody can predict the future. Today you may have a great job, but next year you may be out of a job. Or perhaps an elderly parent may need to live with your family. Or maybe your spouse will decide to stop working and go back to school too. The future is uncertain, which means if something should happen to your finances during the year, you will want to be able to approach the financial aid office to ask for some help. Your best chance of getting help will depend on whether or not you have applied for financial aid. Without having a FAFSA on record, the college has no idea how much of an impact your family has sustained. It makes it much easier for a financial aid officer to give you more money if you have already filled out the FAFSA regardless of whether or not you were given any aid. So think of applying for aid as added insurance against any unexpected changes in your future finances.

237.

If you need more don't be shy to ask for a re-evaluation

If you feel that the amount of financial aid that you are offered by a college is simply nowhere near enough, you can ask for a re-evaluation. For the re-evaluation to be effective you need to provide the financial aid office with concrete reasons why their initial assessment was wrong. Start with an email or call to the financial aid office. Be sure that you have all of your documents ready, and remember that the squeaky wheel gets the grease. If you don't say anything about your package, the college will assume that you are happy with it. We have a special chapter that is dedicated to asking for a re-evaluation. See Chapter 7 for more details.

238.

Get help completing the FAFSA

If you need help completing the FAFSA, visit the U.S. Department of Education website at http://www.fafsa.ed.gov or call 800-4-FED-AID. The website will take you step by step through the entire process. You may also want to contact the financial aid offices at a few local colleges since many hold free workshops to help students complete the FAFSA.

Borrowing the Money You Need

Investing In Your Education

Going to college is an investment in yourself, and often you will need to borrow some money to pay for this investment. Fortunately, there are many places that are willing to lend you money, often on very generous terms. We'll begin by looking at traditional student loans and then investigate a few lesser-known places to borrow money.

For most of us a student loan will be the best and cheapest way to borrow money–unless of course we have the option of an interest-free loan from rich Aunt Emma. To qualify for a student loan you need to apply for financial aid by filling out the Free Application for Federal Student Aid (FAFSA). When you submit the FAFSA, you not only check if you qualify for grant money but you also establish your eligibility to receive government-backed low-interest loans.

There are two types of Federal student loans: subsidized and unsubsidized. For subsidized loans, the government pays the interest on your loan while you are in school so that interest doesn't accrue during that time. For unsubsidized loans, interest accrues while you are in school and you'll end up paying that interest once you start repayment. Whether a loan is subsidized or unsubsidized does not affect when you need to start paying back your loans; it only affects how much interest accrues while you are in school.

Besides Federal student loans there are also private student loans. Like their Federal cousins they often have flexible repayment plans that do not start until after you graduate. The big difference is that the interest rate on a private loan is often based on your credit score and may adjust each year. This can be good if rates go down or bad if rates rise.

Let's take a look at how loans can help with the experience of one student, Diane Glosson.

Diane's Story

Diane Glosson had just ended a 20-year marriage. While most people in her situation would remain near familiar friends and family, she made the radical decision to return to school and eventually left her home in the Midwest to head to Hollywood.

Now 50 years old, Diane has successfully completed her B.A. in cinema television from the University of Southern California. She was only able to afford her education by taking advantage of $22,000 in student loans. Not worried about her newly acquired debt, she intends to take full advantage of her degree when repaying her school loan.

But Diane did not always aspire to be in the entertainment industry. When she began her schooling at Pasadena City College she majored in design. "I wanted to be more creative," she explains. "I took drawing classes and discovered I loved to draw, paint and make models so I switched my major to product design."

As Diane began to include general education courses into her curriculum she discovered even more about herself. "I found I loved psychology, women's history, ethics, the study of Eastern culture and history," she says. "Taking these college classes was the first time in my life I could take what I wanted to take, learn what I wanted to learn. I could do whatever my heart desired."

Diane felt liberated.

After taking a general education class in early film, she became fascinated by the film industry and wanted to be a part of it. "I saw the movie 'High Noon,'" she explains. "I was fascinated that this film was really about McCarthy and the Hollywood blacklist and not a Western at all." The experience was eye opening for Diane. "I decided then and there that we really don't need a better pair of Nike tennis shoes, which is what I was learning in product design. What we really need are movies that make us think about the world around us and what is really going on."

But a degree in cinema meant changing colleges to the University of Southern California, which was not only one of the pre-eminent colleges in the field but also one of the most expensive.

Diane's road that ultimately led to USC began many years before when she was 16 years old and realized that she wanted to go to college. Unfortunately, her family did not have the money to send both her and her brother to school. "No one at New Haven High had ever talked to me about financial aid. I didn't even know it was an option then," she remembers. With only enough money to pay for one child's tuition, her parents opted to send her brother to college, reasoning that he would have to eventually provide for a family. That was the end of Diane's college dreams as she went on to have children and work full-time.

Eventually her husband bought the family business and Diane became the controller, taking seven years to computerize the company and get it in order. While she was happy with what she had accomplished, she approached her husband and told him that she wanted to return to school. His answer was a flat "no." "I had a strong craving to learn and grow and my dreams weren't in the field of accounting," she says.

Diane did return to school, but at a cost that was more than just monetary. "Seeing that I had to divorce my husband to make my dream come true, it was a terribly difficult decision to make," she admits. Going back to school meant getting out of the small town in Indiana where she lived since colleges there did not offer the courses she needed. She left behind her family, friends and even her children, whom she refused to force to move with her.

"I cried every night over the loss of my children and today I still cry for those special moments that I missed with them," she says. But Diane knew that she had to fulfill her dream and eventually, be an example to her children. "We always preached to our children that they would go to college, yet neither my husband nor I had a degree," she says.

Diane's first challenge was finding the money she needed to pay for USC. She received some financial aid while still at the community college in Pasadena, but she continued to use her credit cards in order to live.

"The two years at USC were a constant battle," Diane remembers. At USC she received a package of Stafford loans, in-house scholarships and Perkins loans. Her loans included $2,000 in an AES Student Loan, $2,000 in an AFSA Student Loan which she received through USC, $3,500 in Sallie Mae Stafford loans for the first semester, $4,000 in Sallie Mae Stafford loans for the second semester, $5,500 in Sallie Mae Stafford loans for the third semester and (finally!) $5,000 in Sallie Mae Stafford loans for the fourth semester.

At times all of this borrowing seemed strange for the life she had to adopt. She remembers only getting two hours of sleep because she was up drawing all night for a project or being in the graphics lab until it closed in the wee hours in junior college. At USC she worked in the edit bays until she was kicked out, sometimes at 3 a.m., only a few hours before her 9 a.m. classes. However, about the experience, she says, "I wouldn't have traded a moment of it for anything. Every time I overcame something it just made me more determined and stronger; I knew I could survive anything."

From her experience paying for college, Diane has lessons to share. First, she wishes that she had known the rules better when it came to applying for financial aid. She thought she would be penalized if she owned a home and asked for aid but found that she wasn't. Second, she suggests that you apply for all the scholarships you can find. She says, "It's free money that does not have to be repaid." She reasons that when you graduate you will probably start at an entry-level job with entry-level pay even if you are experienced in other areas, which means that you should take advantage of free money while you have access to it. And she has one last piece of advice for any student thinking of going to school in Los Angeles. She says, "Don't bring out a new car. Odds are it will be wrecked and the car insurance is outrageous!"

Diane is now working as an associate producer at a documentary film company and is proud of having overcome the challenges to get her degree. "When I was in Indiana I was constantly told that my ideas were hair brain, but when I went to school I was rewarded for thinking outside of the box. School has forever changed me," she says.

Student Loan Programs

239.

The Federal Perkins Loans

The Perkins loan is a guaranteed loan carrying a 5 percent interest rate for both undergraduate and graduate students with "exceptional" financial need. The U.S. Department of Education provides colleges with a specific amount of funding, and the schools determine which students have the greatest need. Schools usually add their own funds to the federal funds they receive. To be eligible for this loan you must complete the FAFSA. You do not need to start paying back a Perkins loan until nine months after you graduate, leave school or attend less than half-time. Also, during the time you are in college you do not accumulate any interest on the loan.

240.

The William D. Ford Federal Direct Loans

Direct loans are some of the most common low-interest loans for undergraduate and graduate students. You need to attend an accredited school at least half-time in order to qualify and must use the money only to cover qualified expenses such as tuition and fees, room and board, books and supplies, transportation and living expenses. The Direct loans have a fixed interest rate of 3.76 percent for undergraduate study and 5.31 percent for graduate study. What makes the Direct loans so popular is that they are guaranteed by the government. This means that even if you have low or no credit because the loan is guaranteed by rich Uncle Sam, you'll have no problem getting this loan. There are both subsidized and unsubsidized Direct loans.

241.

The Nursing Student Loan
This is a fixed-rate, low-interest and need-based federal loan. You must be enrolled at least half-time in a program leading to a diploma, associate's, bachelor's or graduate degree in nursing. The amount that you may borrow varies by institution. The interest rate is 5 percent and is subsidized while you are in school. The term of the loan is normally up to 10 years. To apply for this loan, contact the financial aid office at the school where you plan to attend or where you are enrolled.

242.

Health Professions Student Loan (HPSL)
This loan is for financially needy students in the health professions, which include dentistry, optometry, pharmacy, podiatric medicine and veterinary medicine. Individual colleges select loan recipients based on financial need, which is determined from your application for financial aid. The interest rate is fixed at 5 percent. Repayment of the loan begins one year after graduation and is normally for a term of up to 10 years. There is no origination fee and no penalty for early repayment. To apply for this loan, contact the financial aid office at the school where you intend to apply or where you are enrolled.

243.

Loan for Disadvantaged Students (LDS)

This program provides a low-interest 5 percent loan for financially needy students from disadvantaged backgrounds who are pursuing degrees in allopathic medicine, osteopathic medicine, dentistry, optometry, podiatric medicine, pharmacy or veterinary medicine. Individual colleges select loan recipients based on financial need, which is determined from your application for financial aid. The term of the loan is normally up to 10 years. Repayment of the loan begins one year after you graduate. To apply for this loan, contact the financial aid office at the school where you intend to apply or where you are enrolled.

244.

Primary Care Loan (PCL)

This is a low-interest loan of 5 percent for students with financial need who are in the health professions, which include allopathic or osteopathic medicine. Medical students must agree to complete their residency training in primary care within four years after graduation and to practice in primary care for the entire term of the loan. Repayment of the loan begins one year after you graduate, and the term is normally up to 10 years. To apply for this loan, contact the financial aid office at the school where you intend to apply or where you are enrolled.

245.

PLUS Loan for Graduate and Professional Degree Students

This loan program allows graduate and professional degree students to borrow up to the cost of attendance minus other financial aid received. The terms are the same as the Parent Loan for Undergraduate Students. Recipients must not have an adverse credit history, and repayment begins on the date of the last disbursement.

246.

Lower your monthly payments with a Consolidation Loan

It is very likely that you will borrow from more than one student loan program or take out an additional loan during the course of college or graduate school. Having multiple loans means that each month you have to make payments for each loan. It sometimes makes sense to consolidate your federal student loans into a single loan. This makes it easier to pay since you only make a single payment. Also, if you find that the total monthly payments are difficult to make, a consolidation loan can extend the amount of time that you repay the loan, which will lower your monthly payments. Although you will end up paying more interest over the entire life of the loan, you might find that cutting your monthly payments by a third or more is worth it.

You may consolidate Federal Perkins Loans, Federal Unsubsidized and Subsidized Direct Loans, Federal Family Education Loans (FFEL), PLUS Loans, Health Professions Student Loans, Health Education Assistance Loans, Loans for Disadvantaged Students and Federal Nursing Student Loans. The term of your new consolidation loan will be based on your total education debt and the interest rate will be the weighted average of the loans being consolidated, rounded up to the nearest 1/8th of a percent.

> **Is there an easy way to figure out how much my loan really costs and also how much I will have to pay each month once I begin repayment after I graduate?**
>
> The best way to figure out how much you need to pay each month is to use an online loan payment calculator. We like the Repayment Estimator at www.studentloans.gov. On the website, search for "Repayment Estimator." This calculator not only shows you what your monthly payments will be, but it also shows you how much total interest you'll pay. This interest is really the cost of your loan.

You can use the following website to enter your student loans and see how much you can lower your monthly payments and at what cost if you consolidated your student loans: http://www.studentloans.gov.

247.

Lower your interest rate by taking advantage of the Consolidation Loan loophole

If you are in school or still in your grace period, which is the time between when you graduate and when your first loan payment is due, you may be able to consolidate your loan and lower your interest rate. This works because the interest rate while you are in school or during the grace period is often slightly lower than when you begin your repayment period. Therefore, by consolidating while you are still in this lower interest rate period you basically get to extend this lower interest rate throughout the lifetime of the loan.

248.

Choose a loan that offers the best "borrower benefits"

If you need to borrow more than what you're able to through the government, you may want to consider private student loans. If you do, the biggest choice you'll have to make is from whom to borrow the money. In fact, you'll probably find that you have a bunch of banks lining up to offer you money. While money is the same regardless of which bank you choose, you want to be a smart shopper by taking advantage of what are known as "borrower benefits."

As a loan borrower you can get valuable benefits for choosing one bank over another. Often these benefits are money-saving incentives for things such as making on-time payments, making payments via auto-debit or signing up for other services provided by the bank or loan servicer. These incentives may come in the form of partial interest rate reductions or even reductions to the principal balance of your outstanding loans. Usually, you won't need to change anything about the way you repay your loans when an incentive is applied to your account. The monthly payment amount remains the same, and you save money by repaying your loan balance more quickly.

So when you are trying to decide where to get your loan from, compare borrower benefits and then choose the loan that gives you the best benefits.

249.

Make repayment of your loans easier by choosing the right repayment plan

One of the flexibilities of federal student loans is how you can structure repayment. The basic plan is the *standard repayment plan* with a fixed monthly amount for a term of up to 10 years depending on the size of the loan. Smaller loans are usually paid off in less than 10 years. Besides the standard repayment plan you can also select three alternatives. Each of them lengthens the term of the loan and therefore the total amount of interest that you will pay but lowers the monthly payment:

The extended repayment plan. This plan basically extends the term of the loan to 25 years. Doing so will reduce your monthly payments but will result in your paying more in interest. The extended repayment plan may be a good option if you end up borrowing a large amount of money that would make your monthly payments under the standard plan too high. You may opt for the fixed plan, which offers a fixed rate for the full term, or the graduated plan, in which payments increase every two years.

The graduated repayment plan. This plan has a ten-year repayment period. Your initial payments are smaller, and payments are gradually increased every two years over the term of the loan. This method might be helpful when you first graduate since it increases your payments as your salary grows.

The income-driven repayment plans. These plans set your monthly payments according to your income, family size and total amount due. Payments are adjusted each year as your income goes up or down and may be as low as $0 per month. The term of this loan is up to 25 years, and at the end of 25 years, any remaining balance on the loan is discharged.

You can switch from one repayment plan to another once a year as long as the maximum loan term for the new plan is longer than the amount of time you have left under the current plan.

250.

Put all your loan payments on hold using deferment

Under certain situations you can put a hold on all payments of your student loan. If you have a subsidized Direct loan, the government will continue to make the interest payments for you during deferment. If you have an unsubsidized Federal Direct loan, you will still be responsible for all interest that accrues during deferment. To qualify for deferment you must meet one of the following requirements:

- You decide to go back to school at least half-time.
- You become unemployed.
- You are experiencing severe economic hardship.
- You enter into a graduate fellowship program.
- You are involved in rehabilitation training.

Deferment does not mean that you don't ever have to repay your loan, but it gives you a break from making payments. Once your deferment period has ended, you need to resume making your monthly payments.

251.

During tough times reduce the burden of loan payments through forbearance

Forbearance allows you to temporarily postpone your payments, extend the time you have to make payments or make smaller payments for a certain amount of time. You must apply to your lender for forbearance, and they will make the decision on whether to grant your request. If granted you will still be responsible for all interest that accrues during the forbearance period.

Typical circumstances under which a lender may grant forbearance include:

- If you encounter "personal problems" or economic hardship that affects your ability to make your regular payments.
- If you are unemployed and have already used the maximum time allowed for deferment.
- If you have poor health or a disability.

Other situations that will allow you to receive forbearance include:

- Your debt amount exceeds your total monthly income.
- You file for bankruptcy.
- You are serving in a public service organization such as AmeriCorps.
- There is a natural disaster.
- There is a local or national emergency.
- You are completing a medical or dental internship or residency.
- You must serve in the military.

These are not the only reasons you may be granted forbearance. Almost any legitimate reason that makes it difficult for you to pay may qualify for forbearance. Consult with your lender or loan servicer if you encounter any special circumstances that make it difficult for you to make your monthly payments.

252.

There are few legitimate ways to cancel a student loan

You may dream that your loans would be miraculously forgiven, but there are really only a few special circumstances when this can happen. Federal student loan debt is cancelled entirely if a student loan borrower becomes totally and permanently disabled or dies. Other conditions in which student loan debt may be discharged either partially or in full include bankruptcy filing, school closure, false loan certification or an unpaid refund from the school. As you can see you really don't want any of these conditions to befall you in order to cancel your student loan.

253.

Borrow as little as possible

It's tempting to borrow the full amount that you are offered so that you have a little extra spending cash. Resist this temptation! Remember that every dollar that you borrow you will need to repay with interest. Only borrow what you need.

254.

Save money by paying off your loans as early as possible

If you want to save money on your loans, remember that time is your enemy. The longer you hold a loan, the more in interest payments you'll have to make. Consider the following example. Imagine that you borrow $20,000 at 3.76 percent interest. The term of the loan is 10 years. If you made your regular payments, at the end of 10 years you will have paid a total of $24,026, which means you will have paid $4,026 in interest. Now let's assume that you pay a little extra each month so that you end up paying off your loan in eight years. If you did this you would have paid a total of $23,190, or $3,190 in interest, which is a savings of $836. The opposite is also true. If it takes you longer to pay off a loan or if you extend your loan repayment, you will end up paying more in total interest payments.

All federal student loans allow you to pay off the entire loan balance early without any penalties.

255.

Defaulting on a loan will haunt you for a very long time

Defaulting on any student loan is not a good idea. If you start to miss your monthly payments your loan may go into default. This will affect your credit rating and make it hard for you to take out a consumer loan, car loan, mortgage or even pass a simple credit check when renting an apartment. You will also not be eligible to receive any form of financial aid. Defaulted loans can be used to garnish your wages, subtracting up to 10 percent of your salary to pay for your loan. If you are unable to make your scheduled payments, call your lender immediately. There are often steps that can be taken to avoid defaulting.

Keep in mind that a student loan is a serious commitment. Someone trusts you enough to lend you money to pay for your education. In return they expect to be repaid according to the terms of your loan. Take this responsibility seriously.

Private Student Loans

When paying for college, you may find that you need more than what you are offered in federal loans. You may want to consider private student loans. There are also loans that are not specifically designed to pay for college but that still may make sense to use. Let's take a look at some of these private loans.

256.

Take advantage of a private student loan

Many banks and financial institutions offer special loans for students. These typically mirror the federal student loans. However, since they are private loans and not guaranteed by the government, their terms are set by the individual lenders. These loans can be extremely useful if you exhaust your federal sources of aid. Plus, since they are private loans you may apply for them at any time during the school year.

You apply for these loans directly with your lender. The interest rate will often be based on your credit history. The better your credit the lower your interest rate. Most private loans allow you to defer your interest and principal payments until after you graduate. When selecting a private loan, compare the interest rates, repayment options, loan terms and borrower benefits.

257.

Use your home equity to pay for college

If you own your home you may be able to use your home's equity to pay for college. Basically, a home equity loan allows you to use the equity in your home as collateral. You can borrow a lump sum and make monthly payments or you can establish a line of credit and borrow money as you need it.

When you establish a line of credit you only pay the interest on the amount of money that you actually borrow. Interest rates can either be fixed or variable depending on the loan.

Home equity loans have some major advantages over other types of consumer borrowing. For one, you get to deduct interest from your taxes. Even more important may be the fact that borrowing what you need when you need it will not impact your assets as much as taking it all in one lump sum. This means that a home equity line of credit should have less of an impact on your ability to get financial aid. The lower impact that a home equity line of credit has on your assets combined with the tax deduction you get for interest paid makes this one of the better private loans to use to pay for college.

258.

Why you may want to avoid a second mortgage

Some students consider taking out a second mortgage on their home and using the money to pay for college. The problem is that when you receive the loan that entire amount is added to your assets, which will negatively impact your chances for financial aid. A home equity loan with a line of credit, on the other hand, avoids this problem since you only borrow what you need as you need it. This will impact your assets less than a second mortgage. The one risk of a home equity line of credit is that the interest rate is usually variable instead of fixed, but if you are trying to choose between a second mortgage and a home equity line of credit, weigh carefully any impact that receiving all that money will have on your financial aid package.

Can I ever get my student loan totally forgiven?

There are two ways to get your student loan forgiven: the good way and the bad way. The good way is through a loan repayment program (see Chapter 14.) The other way is through default, which is essentially like declaring bankruptcy. If you default on your loan, your credit record will be affected and you will have major difficulty borrowing money in the future. The bank may also decide to take part of your wages to force you to repay your loan.

259.

Borrow from your whole-life insurance policy before you're gone

If you have a whole-life insurance policy as opposed to a term-life policy you may have built up some cash value that you can borrow against. Usually your beneficiaries would receive this cash value after you die, but some policies let you withdraw some of this money or borrow against it. Just remember that unless you pay it back, this amount is taken from your death benefits, decreasing the amount that your beneficiaries receive.

260.

Dip into your IRA penalty-free

You can make withdrawals from your traditional IRAs, Roth IRAs and SIMPLE IRAs and avoid the 10 percent early withdrawal penalty if you use the funds for qualified educational expenses. You will still have to pay income tax on the amount. We recommend that you save this as a last resort because there are other ways to borrow money to pay for school, but there is no such thing as a retirement loan.

261.

If you can stomach the risk you can borrow money from your 401k plan

If you have a 401k retirement plan you can borrow money from it and repay yourself the principal and interest within a five-year period. The risk is that if you lose your job you will have to repay the loan immediately or else face the double whammy of income tax and a penalty on the amount you borrowed.

262.

Borrow money from rich relatives

We all dream of having a rich aunt or uncle who becomes our bene-factor. If you are really lucky, that relative likes you enough to let you have or borrow some money to pay for school. The cleanest way is for them to gift you the money, and they can gift up to $14,000 per year without tax consequences. (In return you will owe them a lifetime worth of gratitude.)

Unfortunately, not all relatives are comfortable just giving away money. You might be able to arrange for a private loan with either no or low interest. Be careful since loans over $10,000 must follow IRS rules on the minimum interest charged and there are tax im-plications for both the lender and borrower. Even more dangerous is the effect a per-sonal loan can have on family relations. What happens if you miss a payment or can't pay back all the money? How will you feel at the next family gathering when you have to face the relative whose loan you are having trouble paying back? All of this can lead to strained family relationships.

If you are going to borrow money that you intend to pay back with interest, it is best to put all of the terms in writing. Include when you should begin repayment–usually sometime after you graduate and can find a job–as well as the consequences of missing a payment–usually a penalty fee.

263.

Have your parents write a check to the college

If you want to avoid the estate tax implications of receiving a large gift of cash from a parent you can have mom or dad write the check directly to the college. Doing so allows them to avoid any estate tax consequences. Even if they write a check for the entire cost of your tuition they will not face any estate taxes as long as the check is made directly to the college. Now the only question is, do you have parents who are in a position to be this charitable?

264.

In a pinch get some emergency cash from your college

Most colleges have money for students who are in a dire emergency. They can arrange for a quick loan to cover an unexpected financial shortfall. A college usually requires that the loan be paid back by the end of the semester or year. However, depending on your circumstances you may be able to negotiate different terms. Visit your financial aid office if you think you need some emergency cash.

Money from Your State

Getting Money From Your State Government

You may not like it when every time you buy something the state tacks on an extra 4 to 8 percent in sales tax. But you can take some consolation in the fact that you may get back some of these dollars through financial aid programs offered by your state. Every state has an agency that helps students pay for college. Many states also administer their own centralized financial aid and scholarship programs. Your state agency is a clearinghouse not only for information but also for actual dollars for college.

Your first step is to find your state agency from the following list and visit their website. On their website you will learn about a variety of assistance programs including scholarships offered by the state. You can also contact the agency directly by phone.

Whether you are surfing their website or speaking to an actual person, your goal is to learn about all of the opportunities available to you. While every state operates differently and not all have the same programs, we have included an overview of the most common programs and resources that you should inquire about.

Jacqueline's Story

Jacqueline Rodriguez graduated with honors from California State University-Los Angeles at the age of 41. While an accomplishment in itself, Jacqueline did so despite being disabled for the past 18 years with both rheumatoid arthritis and lupus.

Jacqueline had always wanted to complete her degree, but soon after high school she got married and quit college. Nevertheless, a college degree was always in the back of her mind. "I knew I could never work a 40-hour a week job because of my disability, but I still needed to bring in an income," she explains. "The only way to do that is to have more education."

But her education had to be put on hold for the time being. Jacqueline and her husband divorced, which made her a single parent. "My emphasis was putting food on the table, paying the bills, working with my disability and raising a son by myself. I didn't have the energy, much less the money, to go back," she explains.

Despite the hardships of her disability and working to support her family, Jacqueline never lost sight of her dream to return to school. Eventually, she was able to scrape together the resources to return to school at the age of 37 after her health forced her to leave her job as an office manager.

Jacqueline's first year in college was not easy. The only financial aid she was able to receive was student loans. This was because her tax return from the prior year had reflected too high of an income. But while her tax return might have shown a nice income, she says, "The financial aid department did not look at the current situation. On paper it looked good, but in reality it wasn't." Jacqueline had no choice but to take out $10,000 in student loans.

Fortunately, Jacqueline also turned to the state for help. She researched various options and applied through a special state program for rehabilitation immediately after she resigned from her job to return to school. It took seven months for the state to approve her application, but once she was approved the program took care of her tuition, books, parking and, in some cases, she received a clothing allowance. The money from the state was a lifesaver and allowed her to graduate with a bachelor's degree in political science without having to take out any additional student loans.

Jacqueline advises other adults to be persistent and not to take "no" for an answer. She says that the key to getting money is to be both resourceful and knowledgeable. She says, "If one person says 'no' then go to the next person until you have exhausted all avenues."

Now that she has successfully completed her degree, Jacqueline laughs as she explains that the absolute hardest thing about returning to school is learning to use your brain again. "With work I just did my best while I was there, but when I left at 5 o'clock that was it," she says. "With school I was not able to rest because I was determined, I wanted to graduate with honors and I wanted to do it the right way."

Jacqueline also says the age difference bothered her somewhat because her classmates in school were so much younger than she. "I would walk into class," she says "and they would stand up at attention because they thought I was the professor." After a while she got used to it, but the first two quarters were uncomfortable.

While most people assumed that getting her undergraduate degree would be the end of the story, for Jacqueline it is just the beginning. She has already begun on her next goal, to earn a master's in social work.

What Your State Offers

When you approach your state agency for higher education you should ask about the following programs. Not all states offer the same programs or resources, but you don't want to miss anything.

State Scholarships and Grants

Many states award their own state scholarships and grants. Make sure you understand how the scholarships work, who is eligible and if you need to apply by a certain deadline. Depending on your state there may be grants specifically for adults students, students who recently received their GED, vocational and technical school students and, of course, undergraduate and graduate school students. Some of these grants will be need-based while others will have no bearing on your financial situation. In some cases all you need to do is file an application to claim your money.

Private Scholarship List

As a clearinghouse for all things related to paying for college, many state agencies also maintain a list of private scholarships that are available to students. On some of the state websites we have found invaluable information including lists of all local civic groups that award scholarships.

State Loan Repayment Programs

Your state might sponsor valuable loan repayment programs depending on what you plan to study. Some states, for example, will help you pay back your student loan if you enter specific career areas such as teaching, law enforcement, medicine, nursing or technology. As long as you work within those fields in the state after graduation, the state will help you pay back your student loans.

State Work-Study

Like Federal Work-Study some states have their own work-study programs. These programs subsidize your salary as you work either on campus or for a government or non-profit agency. Through work-study you can earn thousands of extra dollars while you go to school.

Tuition Exchange

Some states or state university systems have agreements with other states or specific universities in other states to let each other's residents attend at in-state or heavily discounted rates. Paying in-state rates at another state's school can save you thousands of dollars. Often these agreements are made with neighboring states.

Tuition Equalization Grants

These programs are designed to help shrink the difference in the cost of tuition between public and private universities. In Georgia, for example, residents who attend a more expensive private college can qualify to receive a tuition equalization grant of up to $1,045 per year.

Retraining Grants

Some state agencies administer retraining programs for workers who have been laid off. These programs specifically target adults who intend to go back to school to learn a new trade or skill that will help them find employment. In Minnesota, for example, more than 1,300 laid-off workers received training grants worth $4.3 million. The money was distributed through the Minnesota Jobs Skills Partnership Board. If you are going back to school to get a better job, you should inquire about retraining and displaced workers grants.

Disability Grants

Most states offer financial assistance to students who are disabled. The programs vary from state to state as do the qualifications for being classified as disabled. However, if you are disabled you should begin investigating this option early since it can take several months or even a year to get certified for the appropriate program.

Senior Citizen Discounts

If you're over 60, in some states you not only get discounts on dinner but you also get to take college courses at a significant discount or even for free! Check with both your state agency as well as your university to find out what kind of discounts are available to senior citizens.

Other Funding Resources and Services

Be sure to ask about all of the other resources and services that your state offers. Some sponsor workshops to help families apply for financial aid while others have their own publications that they will send you for free on how to pay for college.

It's important that you learn all that you can about the various programs offered by your state. Request all of the free information that they offer and take advantage of any resources such as lists of community scholarships that they provide.

Now find your state agency and start getting the money you need.

State Aid Programs

265. Alabama
Alabama Commission on Higher Education
P.O. Box 302000
Montgomery, AL 36130-2000
Phone: 334-242-1998
In-state Toll-Free: 800-960-7773
Fax: 334-242-0268
Website: http://www.ache.alabama.gov

266. Alaska
Alaska Commission on Postsecondary Education
P.O. Box 110505
Juneau, AK 99811-0505
Phone: 907-465-2962
Toll-Free: 800-441-2962
Fax: 907-465-5316
TTY: 907-465-3143
Email: customer_service@acpe.state.ak.us
Website: http://alaskadvantage.state.ak.us

267. Arizona
Arizona Commission for Postsecondary Education
Suite 650
2020 North Central Avenue
Phoenix, AZ 85004-4503
Phone: 602-258-2435
Fax: 602-258-2483
Website: https://highered.az.gov

268. Arkansas
Arkansas Department of Higher Education
Five Main Place Building
423 Main Street, Suite 400
Little Rock, AR 72201-3818
Phone: 501-371-2000
Fax: 501-371-2001
Website: http://www.adhe.edu

269. California
California Student Aid Commission
P.O. Box 419027
Rancho Cordova, CA 95741-9027
Phone: 916-526-7590
Toll-Free: 888-224-7268
Fax: 916-526-8004
Email: studentsupport@csac.ca.gov
Website: http://www.csac.ca.gov

270. Colorado
Colorado Department of Higher Education
Suite 1600
1560 Broadway
Denver, CO 80202
Phone: 303-866-2723
Fax: 303-866-4266
Email: executivedirector@dhe.state.co.us
Website: http://highered.colorado.gov

271. Connecticut
Connecticut Department of Higher Education
39 Woodland Street
Hartford, CT 06105-2326
Phone: 860-493-3000
Toll-Free: 800-842-0229
Fax: 860-947-1310
Email: lnegro@ctdhe.org
Website: http://www.ctdhe.org

272. Delaware
Delaware Higher Education Commission
The Townsend Building
401 Federal St, Suite 2
Dover, DE 19901
Phone: 302-735-4120
Toll-Free: 800-292-7935
Fax: 302-739-5894
Email: dhec@doe.k12.de.us
Website: http://www.delawaregoestocollege.org

273. District of Columbia

Office of the State Superintendent
of Education (District of Columbia)
9th Floor
801 1st Street NE
Washington, DC 20001
Phone: 202-727-6436
Toll-Free: 877-485-6751
Fax: 202-727-2019
TTY: 202-727-1675
Email: osse@dc.gov
Website: http://osse.dc.gov

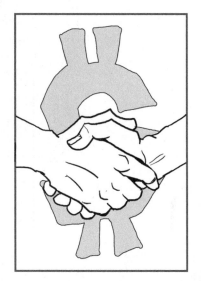

274. Florida

Florida Department of Education
Office of Student Financial
Assistance
325 West Gaines Street, Suite 1314
Tallahassee, FL 32399-0040
Toll-Free: 888-827-2004
Email: osfa@fldoe.org
Website: http://www.floridastudentfinancialaid.org

275. Georgia

Nonpublic Postsecondary Education Commission
2082 East Exchange Place
Suite 220
Tucker, GA 30084-5305
Phone: 770-414-3300
Website: https://gnpec.org

276. Hawaii

Hawaii State Postsecondary Authorization Program
Department of Commerce and Consumer Affairs
Room 310
335 Merchant Street
Honolulu, HI 96813
Phone: 808-586-7327
Fax: 808-956-5158
http://cca.hawaii.gov/hpeap

Hawaii Department of Education
The department publishes an annual Scholarship and Financial Aid Bulletin.
http://www.hawaiipublicschools.org

277. Idaho
Idaho State Board of Education
P.O. Box 83720
Boise, ID 83720-0037
Phone: 208-332-6800
Fax: 208-334-2632
Email: board@osbe.idaho.gov
Website: http://sde.idaho.gov

278. Illinois
Illinois Student Assistance Commission
1755 Lake Cook Road
Deerfield, IL 60015-5209
Phone: 847-948-8500
Toll-Free: 800-899-4722
Fax: 847-831-8549
TTY: 800-526-0844
Email: isac.studentservices@isac.illinois.gov
Website: http://www.isac.org

279. Indiana
Indiana Commission for Higher Education
Suite 300
101 West Ohio Street
Indianapolis, IN 46204-1984
Phone: 317-464-4400
Fax: 317-464-4410
Email: tlubbers@che.in.gov
Website: http://www.che.in.gov

280. Iowa
Iowa College Student Aid Commission
Third Floor
430 E. Grand Avenue
Des Moines, IA 50319
Phone: 515-725-3400

Toll-Free: 877-272-4456
Fax: 515-725-3401
Email: info@iowacollegeaid.org
Website: http://www.iowacollegeaid.gov

281. Kansas

Kansas Board of Regents
Curtis State Office Building
Suite 520
1000 SW Jackson Street
Topeka, KS 66612-1368
Phone: 785-296-3421
Fax: 785-296-0983
Website: http://www.kansasregents.org

282. Kentucky

Kentucky Higher Education Assistance Authority
100 Airport Road
Frankfort, KY 40602-0798
Phone: 502-696-7200
Toll-Free: 800-928-8926
Fax: 502-696-7496
TTY: 800-855-2880
Email: studentaid@kheaa.com
Website: http://www.kheaa.com

283. Louisiana

Louisiana Office of Student Financial Assistance
602 North Fifth Street
Baton Rouge, LA 70802
Phone: 225-219-1012
Toll-Free: 800-259-5626 x 1012
Fax: 225-208-1496
Email: custserv@la.gov
Website: http://www.osfa.state.la.us

284. Maine

Maine Education Assistance Division
Finance Authority of Maine (FAME)
P.O. Box 949
Augusta, ME 04332-0949
Phone: 207-623-3263

Toll-Free: 800-228-3734
Fax: 207-213-2661
TTY: 207-626-2717
Email: education@famemaine.com
Website: http://www.famemaine.com

285. Maryland
Maryland Higher Education Commission
6 N. Liberty Street
Baltimore, MD 21201
Phone: 410-767-3301
In-state Toll-Free: 800-974-0203
Fax: 410-260-3200
TTY: 800-735-2258
Website: http://www.mhec.state.md.us

286. Massachusetts
Massachusetts Department of Higher Education
Room 1401
One Ashburton Place
Boston, MA 02108-1696
Phone: 617-994-6950
Fax: 617-727-6397
Email: cmccurdy@osfa.mass.edu
Website: http://www.mass.edu

287. Michigan
Michigan Student Financial Services Bureau
P.O. Box 30047
Lansing, MI 48909-7547
Toll-Free: 800-642-5626 x37054
Fax: 517-241-0155
Email: sfs@michigan.gov
Website: http://www.michigan.gov/mistudentaid

288. Minnesota
Minnesota Office of Higher Education
Suite 350
1450 Energy Park Drive
Saint Paul, MN 55108-5227
Phone: 651-642-0567
Toll-Free: 800-657-3866

Fax: 651-642-0675
TTY: 800-627-3529
Email: larry.pogemiller@state.mn.us
Website: http://www.ohe.state.mn.us

289. Mississippi
Mississippi Institutions of Higher Learning
3825 Ridgewood Road
Jackson, MS 39211-6453
Phone: 601-432-6623
In-state Toll-Free: 800-327-2980
Fax: 601-432-6972
Email: commissioner@ihl.state.ms.us
Website: http://www.ihl.state.ms.us

290. Missouri
Missouri Department of Higher Education
205 Jefferson Street
P.O. Box 1469
Jefferson City, MO 65102
Phone: 573-751-2361
Toll-Free: 800-473-6757
Fax: 573-751-6635
TTY: 800-735-2966
Email: info@dhe.mo.gov
Website: http://www.dhe.mo.gov

291. Montana
Montana University System
2500 Broadway
P.O. Box 203201
Helena, MT 59620-3201
Phone: 406-444-6570
Fax: 406-444-1469
Website: http://www.mus.edu

292. Nebraska
Nebraska Coordinating Commission for Postsecondary Education
Suite 300
140 North Eighth Street
P.O. Box 95005
Lincoln, NE 68509-5005

Phone: 402-471-2847
Fax: 402-471-2886
Website: https://ccpe.nebraska.gov

293. Nevada

Nevada Department of Education
700 East Fifth Street
Carson City, NV 89701
Phone: 775-687-9200
Fax: 775-687-9101
Website: http://www.doe.nv.gov

294. New Hampshire

New Hampshire Postsecondary Education Commission
101 Pleasant Street
Concord, NH 03301-3860
Phone: 603-271-3494
Fax: 603-271-2696
TTY: 800-735-2964
Website: http://www.education.nh.gov/highered/

295. New Jersey

Office of the Secretary of Higher Education
20 West State Street, 4th Floor
P.O. Box 542
Trenton, NJ 08625-0542
Phone: 609-292-4310
Fax: 609-292-7225
Website: http://www.state.nj.us/highereducation/

Higher Education Student Assistance Authority
P.O. Box 545
Four Quakerbridge Plaza
Trenton, NJ 08625-0545
Phone: 609-584-4480
Toll-Free: 800-792-8670
Fax: 609-588-7389
TTY: 609-588-2526
Website: http://www.hesaa.org

What can I get from my state higher education agency?

Not only is your state agency a clearinghouse for information on state scholarships and financial aid but also for free tips and advice. Most state agencies have an online or print publication that you can get for free. Inside it will detail all of the various state programs along with instructions for applying. When you contact your state agency be sure to request all of the free information it offers.

296. New Mexico
New Mexico Higher Education Department
300 Don Gaspar Avenue
Santa Fe, NM 87501
Phone: 505-827-5800
Toll-Free: 800-279-9777
Fax: 505-476-8453
TTY: 800-659-8331
Email: highered@state.nm.us
Website: http://ped.state.nm.us

Albuquerque Community Foundation (ACF)
P.O. Box 25266
Albuquerque NM 87125-5266
Phone: 505-883-6240
Email: foundation@albuquerquefoundation.org
Website: http://www.albuquerquefoundation.org

297. New York
New York State Higher Education Services Corporation
99 Washington Avenue
Albany, NY 12255
Phone: 518-473-1574
Toll-Free: 888-697-4372
Fax: 518-474-2839
TTY: 800-445-5234
Email: webmail@hesc.org
Website: https://www.hesc.ny.gov

298. North Carolina
North Carolina State Education Assistance Authority
P.O. Box 13663
Research Triangle Park, NC 27709-3663
Phone: 919-549-8614
In-state Toll-Free: 866-866-2362
Fax: 919-549-8481
Email: information@ncseaa.edu
Website: http://www.cfnc.org

299. North Dakota
North Dakota University System
State Student Financial Assistance Program
Department 215
600 East Boulevard Avenue
Bismarck, ND 58505-0230
Phone: 701-328-2960
Fax: 701-328-2961
Email: robin.putnam@ndus.edu
Website: http://www.ndus.edu

300. Ohio
Ohio Board of Regents
University System of Ohio
25 South Front Street
Columbus, OH 43215
Phone: 614-466-6000
Toll-Free: 888-833-1133
Fax: 614-466-5866
Email: hotline@regents.state.oh.us
Website: http://www.ohiohighered.org/board

Ohio Department of Education
25 South Front Street
Columbus, OH 43215-4183
Toll-Free: 877-644-6338
Website: http://www.ode.state.oh.us

301. Oklahoma
Oklahoma State Regents for Higher Education
Suite 200
655 Research Parkway

Oklahoma City, OK 73104
Phone: 405-225-9100
Toll-Free: 800-858-1840
Fax: 405-225-9230
Email: communicationsdepartment@osrhe.edu
Website: http://www.okhighered.org

302. Oregon
Oregon Office of Student Access and Completion
Suite 100
1500 Valley River Drive
Eugene, OR 97401
Phone: 541-687-7400
Toll-Free: 800-452-8807
Fax: 541-687-7414
Email: public_information@mercury.osac.state.or.us
Website: http://www.oregonstudentaid.gov

303. Pennsylvania
Bureau of Postsecondary and Adult Education
State Department of Education
333 Market Street, 12th Floor
Harrisburg, PA 17126
Phone: 717-787-5532
Fax: 717-783-0583
TTY: 717-783-8445
Website: http://www.education.pa.gov

Pennsylvania Higher Education Assistance Agency
Pennsylvania State Grant Program
P.O. Box 8157
Harrisburg, PA 17105-8157
In-state Toll-Free: 800-692-7392
TDD: Dial 711
Website: http://www.pheaa.org

304. Rhode Island
Rhode Island Higher Education Assistance Authority
560 Jefferson Boulevard, Suite 100

Warwick, RI 02886
Phone: 401-736-1100
Toll-Free: 800-922-9855
TTY: 401-734-9481
Email: info@riheaa.org
Website: http://www.riheaa.org

Rhode Island Office of Higher Education
80 Washington Street, Suite 524
Providence, RI 02903
Phone: 401-456-6000
Fax: 401-462-9345
TTY: 401-456-6028
Website: http://www.ribghe.org

305. South Carolina
South Carolina Commission on Higher Education
Suite 300
1122 Lady Street
Columbia, SC 29201
Phone: 803-737-2260
Toll-Free: 877-349-7183
Email: frontdesk@che.sc.gov
Website: http://www.che.sc.gov

306. South Dakota
South Dakota Board of Regents
Suite 200
306 East Capitol Avenue
Pierre, SD 57501
Phone: 605-773-3134
Fax: 605-773-5320
Email: info@sdbor.edu
Website: http://www.sdbor.edu

307. Tennessee
Tennessee Higher Education Commission
Parkway Towers
Suite 1900
404 James Robertson Parkway
Nashville, TN 37243-0830
Phone: 615-741-3605

Fax: 615-741-6230
Email: lovella.carter@state.tn.gov
Website: http://www.tn.gov/thec

308. Texas
Texas Higher Education Coordinating Board
1200 E. Anderson Lane
Austin, TX 78711
Phone: 512-427-6101
Toll-Free: 800-242-3062
Fax: 512-427-6127
Email: grantinfo@thecb.state.tx.us
Website: http://www.thecb.state.tx.us

309. Utah
Utah State Board of Regents
Gateway Center
60 South 400 West
Salt Lake City, UT 84101
Phone: 801-321-7101
Fax: 801-321-7156
Email: jcottrell@utahsbr.edu
Website: http://www.higheredutah.org

310. Vermont
Vermont Student Assistance Corporation
10 East Allen Street
P.O. Box 2000
Winooski, VT 05404-2601
Phone: 802-655-9602
Toll-Free: 800-642-3177
Fax: 802-654-3765
TTY: 800-281-3341
Email: info@vsac.org
Website: http://www.vsac.org

311. Virginia
State Council of Higher Education for Virginia
James Monroe Building
Tenth Floor
101 North 14th Street
Richmond, VA 23219

Phone: 804-225-2600
Fax: 804-225-2604
Email: kirstennelson@schev.edu
Website: http://www.schev.edu

312. Washington
Washington State Achievement Council
917 Lakeridge Way SW
Olympia, WA 98502
Phone: 360-753-7800
Email: info@wsac.wa.gov
Website: http://www.wsac.wa.gov

Office of Superintendent of Public Instruction
Old Capitol Building
P.O. Box 47200
Olympia, WA 98504-7200
Phone: 360-725-6075
TTY: 360-664-3631
Website: http://www.k12.wa.us

313. West Virginia
West Virginia Higher Education Policy Commission
1018 Kanawha Boulevard, East, Suite 700
Charleston, WV 25301
Phone: 304-558-2101
Fax: 304-558-1011
Email: canderson@hepc.wvnet.edu
Website: http://www.wvhepc.edu

314. Wisconsin
Wisconsin Higher Educational Aids Board
Suite 902
131 West Wilson Street
Madison, WI 53707
Phone: 608-267-2206
Fax: 608-267-2808
Email: cassie.weisensel@wisconsin.gov
Website: http://www.heab.state.wi.us

Wisconsin Department of Public Instruction
125 South Webster Street
P.O. Box 7841
Madison, WI 53707-7841
Phone: 608-266-3390
Toll-Free: 800-441-4563
Website: http://dpi.wi.gov

315. Wyoming
Wyoming Community College Commission
Fifth Floor, Suite B
2300 Capitol Avenue
Cheyenne, WY 82002
Phone: 307-777-7144
Fax: 307-777-6567
Email: jrose@commission.wcc.edu
Website: http://www.commission.wcc.edu

Wyoming Department of Education
2300 Capitol Avenue
Hathaway Building, 2nd Floor
Cheyenne, WY 82002-2060
Phone: 307-777-7675
Fax: 307-777-6234
Website: http://edu.wyoming.gov

U.S. Territories

316. American Samoa
American Samoa Community College
Board of Higher Education
P.O. Box 2609
Pago Pago, AS 96799-2609
Phone: 684-699-9155
Email: info@amsamoa.edu
Website: http://www.amsamoa.edu

317. Commonwealth of the Northern Mariana Islands
Northern Marianas Department of Education
CNMI Public School System
Saipan, MP 96950-1250
Phone: 670-237-3027
Fax: 670-234-1270
Email: boe.admin@cnmipss.org
Website: http://www.cnmipss.org

318. Puerto Rico
Puerto Rico Council on Higher Education
P.O. Box 19900
Ave. Ponce de Leon 268
Edificio Hato Rey Center Piso 15
Hato Rey, PR 00918
Phone: 787-641-7100
Fax: 787-641-2573
Email: mi_wiscovich@ces.gobierno.pr
Website: http://www.ce.pr.gov

319. Republic of the Marshall Islands
Republic of the Marshall Islands
RMI Scholarship Grant and Loan Board
P.O. Box 1436
Majuro, MH 96960
Phone: 692-625-5770
Email: misglb@ntamar.net
Website: http://www.rmischolarship.net

320. Virgin Islands

Virgin Islands Department of Education
1834 Kongens Gade
St. Thomas, VI 00802
Phone: 340-774-2810
Fax: 340-779-7153
Email: lterry@doe.vi
Website: http://www.doe.vi

Money from Your College

Money From Your College

Believe it or not but your college is your best ally when it comes to getting money. Sure they charge you for tuition, but they can also give you financial aid, scholarships and grants. Colleges receive money from alumni, community foundations and others to create scholarships for deserving students. And they staff offices with knowledgeable administrators whose job is to help you figure out how to lower the sticker price of your education.

To make paying for college as painless as possible, take advantage of every opportunity and resource that your school offers. In this chapter we will outline the various services your college may offer to give you a road map for how to maximize their assistance.

There are also some ways that you can save money through various programs such as tuition remission and reciprocity agreements between colleges. Some colleges even offer alumni referrals, which can save you a few hundred dollars. All of these may be available at your school.

Finally, you can always ask for more money from your college. Usually this means that you have submitted your financial aid application

but the financial aid package that you receive from the college is just not enough to allow you to pay the tuition bills. If you can present a sound case for why the college's financial aid offer is not sufficient, you may be able to convince the college to give you more assistance.

If you view your college as your partner in making your education affordable, you will be pleasantly surprised an how much help you can receive. Sometimes all you need to do to get some help is to ask!

Stephanie's Story

Stephanie Wilson was a homemaker for nearly two decades before she finally fulfilled her life-long dream of earning a college degree. While it was not easy to go back to school at age 42, the decision, once made, felt like the lifting of a heavy burden.

"It was not easy to trade my life as a full-time mom for that of a student," admits Stephanie. "I had my routine and led a comfortable life. But I always felt that something was missing. When I finally took the plunge and applied to college I felt like my life was moving forward. At that moment I realized I had done the right thing."

Stephanie's sense of joy lasted as long as it took to get the first tuition bill. "When that first bill arrived I suddenly found myself asking 'What have I done?'" recalls Stephanie. Without wasting another day, she scheduled a visit to her school's financial aid office to speak with a counselor.

"What a relief it was to find people who were willing to help," remembers Stephanie after her first appointment. Eventually, Stephanie became a familiar face in the financial aid office and was soon befriending and even having lunch with some of the counselors. "The financial aid counselors often have a thankless job. They hear all of the sad stories of families who can't pay for college and while they try to help as best they can there is never enough money to solve everyone's problem. What most students need to understand is that they are going to have to work and do their part to pay for tuition."

In her case, the financial aid office was able to find a small grant after she completed a financial aid application. But since she did not qualify for a lot of financial aid the counselors recommended that she explore scholarships. Giving her a list of awards to pursue, Stephanie embarked on a mission to win scholarships.

"I made applying for scholarships a job," says Stephanie. "I applied for awards from my department and from the college. I also tracked down civic groups and non-profits. For every scholarship that I applied to I must have seen 20 or 30 that I didn't."

"It was winning that first scholarship—which was worth only $250—that convinced me that I was not wasting my time. Once those checks started to roll in I was a convert and became even more committed to applying for scholarships. Each week I would visit the financial aid office to peruse their books and databases. Everyone in the office knew that I was looking for scholarships and they would always tell me about new ones that they had received information about," says Stephanie.

The financial aid office also helped Stephanie land a part-time job on campus. "While the job did not pay much, it certainly helped," says Stephanie. "Plus, the hours were flexible and my boss knew that school came first. Whenever I had a test I could adjust my hours to let me study more."

Between the small grant from the college, outside scholarships, work and her savings, Stephanie was able to pay for college without borrowing a single dime in student loans.

Stephanie enthusiastically recommends that all students work with their college early to learn about all of the scholarship, grant and financial aid opportunities. Stephanie regrets that she did not start earlier and that it took the shock of the first tuition bill to get her to seek help.

While her path to a degree has not been an easy one, Stephanie can look back on her experience with pride. Not only did she make a life changing decision to go back to college and fulfill a life-long dream, but she did so without overburdening herself (and her family) with debt.

Hitting Up Your College For Money

321.

Start by asking your college about scholarships

Your college is one of the best places to find scholarships. Colleges give both need-based awards to students with low financial means as well as merit-based awards for everything from a student's interests to career goals. The challenge is that these scholarships are often spread throughout the university system. Many scholarships are administered by either the admission or financial aid office. Plus, your own department may also have specific awards for students in your major. To complicate things, various campus groups—such as the school newspaper—may also award scholarships to their members. Make sure you don't leave any stone unturned when looking for resources. As you search for scholarships on your campus be sure to check these places:

- Admission office
- Financial aid office
- Student development office
- Adult learning center
- Career center
- Library
- Alumni clubs
- Student clubs and organizations
- Foundations

Take a look at Chapter 2 for more information on college scholarships. Remember too that the various departments in your college may also maintain lists of scholarships offered by the community and businesses. Be sure to inquire about these lists to save yourself time when searching outside of the campus.

322.

Look for guaranteed college scholarships

We usually say that there is no such thing as a guaranteed scholarship. Scholarships are competitions, which you win based on the quality of your application. However, there are some scholarships that are virtually guaranteed. These awards are usually based on your grades or test scores.

If you have taken the GRE or even the SAT within the past four or five years you may be able to use these scores to qualify for one of these awards. Also, if you have any postsecondary education you may be able to have those grades count as well.

For example, Saint Joseph's College in Rensselaer, Indiana (http://www.saintjoe.edu), offers an *Honors Scholarship* worth up to $17,000 to all accepted students with certain GPAs and test scores. There is a calculator on the website to see if you qualify. For example, you could have an SAT score of 1300 and GPA of 3.25 to win the scholarship.

It is important that you carefully research your current college or colleges that you are applying to and inquire if you can substitute any comparable scores or grades to qualify.

323.

Free scholarships for transfer students

If you are transferring into a college from another school or community college you may qualify for a guaranteed transfer scholarship. For example, Spalding University in Louisville, Kentucky, offers a scholarship for transfer students according to the following scale:

- Up to 50 percent of tuition for students who compete and become *University Scholars*
- 29 percent of tuition for all students with 3.5-4.0 GPAs

- 25 percent of tuition for all students with 3.2-3.49 GPAs
- 22 percent of tuition for all students with 3.0-3.19 GPAs

If you are thinking about transferring, speak with the admission office at the colleges you are considering. Ask them what kind of financial aid package you may expect and inquire about transfer scholarships that you may be eligible to receive.

324.

You might be entitled to a state entitlement award

All states have financial aid programs for their residents. Some of these programs have specific awards for adult and returning students or for students who enter certain fields like nursing, medicine or education. Be aware that some require you to use the money only at colleges within your state. Take a look at Chapter 6 and find your state agencies for higher education. Contact this agency to learn which scholarships are available. Also, ask your college's financial aid office about any state entitlement programs and grants that you can take advantage of to help you pay for tuition.

325.

Get in-state tuition even if you're an out-of-state student

Getting in-state tuition at a public university can save you thousands of dollars. Take a look at the difference in tuition for the University of California at Berkeley. If you are not a resident of California you will have to pay an additional non-resident fee of $26,682 per year.

If you are an out-of-state student you will need to pay out-of-state tuition until you can establish state residency. This is easier in some states than others. Texas, for example, does not like students who move to their state just to use their fine educational system and then leave. One of the residency requirements is that you live in Texas for 12 months without attending a secondary institution.

The University of California system, on the other hand, makes it possible but not easy. To become a resident you need to show three things:

Physical presence. You must have proof that you remained in the state for more than one year. This means not going home for the summer. You actually have to physically be in the state and be able to prove it.

Intent. You must establish ties to the state of California that show you intend to make California your home. This requires giving up any previous residence and getting proof such as a California driver's license.

Financial independence. You qualify if you are at least 24 years old, are a veteran of the U.S. Armed Forces, are a ward of the court or both parents are deceased, have legal dependents besides a spouse, are married or are a single student and have not been claimed as an income tax deduction by your parents for the past year for graduate students or past two years for undergraduate students.

California's rules are fairly common among the states. If you are planning to attend a public college outside of your own state, contact the admission office and make sure you understand what you need to do to get state residency. Once you do you'll save a bundle, and it's just like winning a guaranteed scholarship.

326.

Take advantage of residency discount agreements

Some schools have formed relationships with neighboring states to offer their residents automatic in-state rates from the beginning. The

University of Arkansas, for example, offers a *Non-Resident Tuition Award* for entering freshmen from neighboring states that include Texas, Mississippi, Louisiana, Kansas, Missouri, Oklahoma and Tennessee. This can save you up to $14,000 a year in fees. If you want to attend a state college in a neighboring state, contact the admission office to find out if any such discount agreements are in effect.

327.

Save money with a reciprocity agreement

Some state university systems have buddied up with other state university systems to grant in-state or discounted tuition at each other's schools. These are known as reciprocity agreements and can save you a ton of money. Residents of Colorado, for example, can attend any public university in Hawaii and pay discounted tuition. The same is true for Hawaii residents who attend a Colorado public university.

One of the largest reciprocity programs is the Western Undergraduate Exchange (WUE), coordinated by the Western Interstate Commission for Higher Education. Under this program, students from Alabama, Arizona, California, Colorado, Hawaii, Idaho, Montana, Nevada, North Dakota, Oregon, Utah, Washington and Wyoming may enroll in designated two-year and four-year institutions and programs in other participating states at a cost lower than non-resident tuition. In other words you get a discount! Contact the office of admission at the colleges you want to attend to see what reciprocity agreement may already be in place.

328.

Get a flexible campus job

A college campus is a mini city and there are many jobs that need to be filled by students. From working in the library to being a research assistant for a professor there are part-time jobs of every kind. The best thing about an on-campus job is that it offers you flexibility to fit in with your class schedule. Plus, your boss won't be surprised around final exams when you need to reduce your work hours.

329.

Get started at a less-expensive school and then transfer to graduate from a more-expensive school

As you already know tuition prices vary widely. However, in general most colleges offer similar courses and credits that are transferable from one school to another. With careful planning you can start at a less-expensive school such as a community college and after two years transfer into a more-expensive college while still graduating on time.

A lot of students overlook their local community colleges. Yet it's a great way to complete two years of your education for less than half the price of a four-year college. (Some four-year colleges even offer automatic admission and scholarships to community college students who transfer into their schools.) When it comes time to get a job, potential employers are only interested in where you graduated from, not the path you took to get there.

The key to making this work is to choose a community college, or similarly inexpensive school, where your credits will transfer smoothly. Look for articulation agreements, which are special agreements that colleges set up with one another that specify which classes are equivalent and what credits will transfer. They also outline what it takes to actually transfer schools in terms of grades and other requirements. Make sure that you are transferring into a college that will count all (or at least enough) of the credits you have already earned to allow you to graduate on time. If your credits don't count and you have to repeat courses, you may take longer to graduate and lose any potential savings.

330.

Go to a less-expensive undergraduate college so you can blow your money on an expensive graduate school

If you are planning to get a graduate or professional degree, then consider going to a cheap college and saving your money for graduate school. For example, let's say that you want to be a doctor. You're not going to learn much about brain surgery during your undergraduate years. So why go to an expensive undergraduate college when you can go to a cheaper alternative? Then, if you want to attend the most elite (and expensive) medical school, you will have saved yourself a few clams.

331.

Work and learn through cooperative education programs

Would you like to make college more affordable while gaining valuable work experience? Cooperative education programs, known as co-ops, allow you to work and go to school at the same time. Plus, cooperative education gives you the benefits of having work experience before you graduate and earning a paycheck without missing out on the college experience.

Co-op works because companies, governments and non-profit organizations agree to offer real jobs to students. Job assignments are managed by the college, and students are matched with jobs that fit their major or are in career areas that they wish to explore. Each year more than 50,000 employers hire college co-op students in nearly every field of work.

The best way to learn more about co-op is to speak to the cooperative education office at the college you are attending or plan to attend. Also visit the website of the National Commission for Cooperative Education at http://www.co-op.edu to learn more about co-op education. At the library, look for the *Directory of College Cooperative Education Programs*, which lists the more than 460 colleges that offer co-op programs. With cooperative education you can work while attending college and even graduate with a year or more of actual work experience on your resume.

332.

Take advantage of tuition remission, if you can

If you are an employee or the child of an employee or alumnus of a college you may get a break in your tuition. At Loyola University in Chicago, for example, one of the employee benefits is the Faculty and Staff Children Exchange Program (FACHEX). This gives the children of employees free tuition at Loyola and 25 other Jesuit colleges and universities.

To a lesser extent some colleges also give tuition breaks for the children of alums. At Mississippi State University, for example, students who are the sons or daughters of alumni who must pay out-of-state tuition for graduate school can earn a 50 percent reduction in tuition as long as they maintain a 3.0 GPA. So if you or your parents have any connection to a college, check for a tuition remission program.

333.

Save some money with an alumni referral

Who says colleges don't know how to market themselves? Alumni of the College of St. Catherine in St. Paul and Minneapolis, Minnesota, get free referral cards that they may give to students. These referral cards grant students application fee waivers and one-time tuition discounts of between $300 and $600 if they enroll. If you know graduates of colleges that you want to apply to, ask them to contact their alumni offices about application fee waivers and tuition discounts for referrals.

334.

Pay for tuition monthly instead of in one lump sum

Depending on your cash flow it might be easier to pay for tuition in small amounts each month instead of in one big lump sum at the start of each semester. Some schools allow you to spread your payments over the year instead of paying once or twice a year. Check with the college to see if they offer this type of payment. If your school participates in the TuitionPay monthly payment program, you can pay a small fee to have your tuition divided into payments, with no interest. Currently more than 1,500 schools participate in this plan. To see if your school participates in TuitionPay, visit http://www.tuitionpay.com.

Pam's Story

Pam Lewis is not the type of woman to take "no" for an answer. She was 47 years old when she returned to school to earn her undergraduate degree. In her scholarship essay to the Business and Professional Women's Foundation she wrote, "Going back to school has been a turning point in my life, something I have yearned to do for 30 years. After caring for my in-laws with Alzheimer's, my sons and a disabled husband for 21 years, I discovered a marvelous gift. I recognized my inner strength—a streak of resoluteness that has been my staying power."

Pam has relied on this strength again and again during her pursuit of a college education. It was this strength that also gave her the courage to work with her school to make sure she received the most money possible.

When Pam transferred from Cleveland State Community College to Tennessee Wesleyan College, her academic record made her eligible for the Presidential scholarship. Before she even began at Wesleyan, Pam had received from the financial aid office a letter asking for her signature to accept the Presidential scholarship. However, Pam had done her homework and through her research and conversations with the financial aid office knew that she was also eligible for the Phi Theta Kappa scholarship, which was worth more than the Presidential. But since the college only gave out 10 Phi Theta Kappa awards, She didn't want to turn down the Presidential scholarship since she had no guarantee of winning the Phi Theta Kappa. Pam called the financial aid office and explained her dilemma. To her delight the financial aid office agreed to hold her Presidential scholarship until she found out the results of the Phi Theta Kappa. As it turned out Pam won one of the last Phi Theta Kappa scholarships.

"By asking the financial aid officer," Pam concludes, "I was able to go after the higher paying scholarship, and I ended up getting it."

Pam believes that staying in frequent communication with the advisor of her major and financial aid officers at Wesleyan was the best thing she ever did. Her advisor directed her to specific courses to take for the remainder of her time at community college. In addition, she asked the financial aid office about scholarships, and they helped her make sure she didn't miss out on any since many were on a first come, first served basis.

Pam's path to return to school began when she decided to go for a one-year certificate in an area that would allow her to work from home and still be able to care for her live-in mother-in-law. She went to school in the beginning at night while her husband was at home to share his mother's care.

While she confides that she is a lifelong student, she says it was quite a bit harder to convince her husband to support her to return to school. "He is not the student in life that I am," she says. "He was always thinking of the financial side of the picture." Her argument was that returning to school and receiving her degree would afford her the ability to help supplement their financial resources, alleviate stress from her husband, plan for a long-term future and feed her insatiable appetite for learning.

When Pam first returned to school her husband was working and it made it somewhat easier financially. She had also researched her degree choices and was determined she would not quit until she received a bachelor's degree in human services. She began her studies at the local community college. However, during this time her husband had to go for outpatient surgery, a simple procedure she explains. "He came out never able to work again," she finishes.

Pam was forced to take a year off from school and the family lived off her husband's disability payments, savings and stocks and bonds. When she did return to school she says, "We lived for the next two years very frugally."

Friends and family pitched in to help Pam achieve her dream and she says that her husband has grown accustomed to her taking her schoolbooks in the car when they have to go somewhere. "He goes to bed alone now while I slip in hours later," Pam says. "The home-cooked meals all made from scratch are almost non-existent and sandwiches, eating out or fast foods have become more of the norm," she explains.

It's all worth the sacrifice, Pam believes, "This is a joint venture with joint rewards." Even with the scholarships, she still cuts corners and makes financial shortcuts in order to afford her education. She accepts that her home life might never be the same again, or at least until she completes her education. But even with those challenges, Pam is certain that she has made the right decision to go back to school. "It is undoubtedly worth it," she says, "Not only for the more secure future it provides, but for the growth it has provided for me. I did a lot of research before deciding on the degree and career field I chose and so I am very confident that my degree will prove useful."

After graduating from Tennessee Wesleyan College, Pam intends to begin her graduate studies in social work. Her goal is to work in a small town where she can develop and implement programs for at-risk teens or senior citizens. "I have a deep love for both of these populations and since we have so little resources available in our rural area, the field is ripe and the need is great," she concludes.

335.

Ask for a better financial aid deal

Let's get one thing out of the way. College financial aid officers hate the word "negotiate." Perhaps it's because the word conjures up visions of haggling with a car salesperson over the cost of floor mats. But regardless of the word you use, it is a well-documented fact that colleges have wiggle room when it comes to your financial aid package if there are solid reasons for change. If you approach them in the right way and provide the right evidence, you may be able to lower the sticker price of your education.

But if you can't use the word "negotiate," what do you call bargaining with the colleges? The word that financial aid officers don't mind is "reassessment." Basically this means you ask the financial aid officers to reconsider the financial aid package that they offered. But you can't just ask for a reassessment without a reason. You need to provide financial aid officers with concrete reasons for why you deserve a better financial aid package.

If you look at a typical financial aid offer you'll notice that there are two critical areas that determine how much you get.

1. Your Expected Family Contribution. This is the amount that the college has determined that your family can afford to pay. They arrive at this figure by crunching the numbers that you provide on your financial aid application. Once the college determines how much you can pay, all they need to figure out is how to make up for the gap between what you can pay and what it costs to attend their college.

2. The packaging of your award. Your financial aid offer might consist of a combination of grants, work-study and student loans. The composition of your award–called packaging–makes a big difference. Would you rather get $10,000 in grants or $10,000 in student loans?

Your goal when asking for a "reassessment" is to provide reasons why the Expected Family Contribution is not accurate and makes it extremely difficult or even impossible for you to afford college and/or to increase the amount of grant money in your package. You do this by submitting a letter or scheduling an in-person appointment with the financial aid officer. In your letter or meeting, request a reassessment and provide reasons why the original offer is just not realistic.

The success of your reassessment will depend on the reasons that you give to support your claim that their initial analysis needs fixing. Let's

> **How should I contact the financial aid office to ask for a reassessment?**
>
> Timing is important because financial aid budgets do get depleted. If you are close to the college, you should try to make an in-person appointment. Otherwise, go with email. Sending snail mail just takes too long. You need to give the college time to respond, so the sooner you can let them know of your request for a reassessment the better.

look at some reasons that you can provide to the financial aid office to convince them that they should reassess your financial aid package.

Present any special circumstances not reflected by the numbers in your financial aid application.

All the college sees are the numbers that you provide on your financial aid forms. These numbers are based on your income taxes, which are always two years behind. If something has changed recently that affects your family's finances you need to tell the college. Changes to your family's finances may include:

- Unusual medical expenses
- Unemployment of you or your spouse
- Ongoing divorce or separation
- Care for an aging relative

Whatever the circumstance be sure to explain it in detail in your letter or when you meet with the financial aid officer. Don't just describe the event, but show with numbers how it impacts your family's finances. Financial aid officers like to deal with numbers, which means you need to justify everything with them.

Don't wait for something bad to happen if you know it will.

You don't have to wait until something happens to let the financial aid officer know about it. If you know that there will be a change in your employment or if there will be an unavoidable financial expenditure, let the financial aid office know about it now. Like any large organization the college has a limited budget. If you wait until something happens it might be too late for the college to do anything about it. If you let them know in advance they may be able to budget for it and have the money for you when the inevitable occurs.

Compare financial aid offers.

If you have been accepted to several colleges and receive financial aid packages that are vastly different, you may be able to use one to motivate the other to be a little more generous. Let's imagine that your first choice, College A, gives you a smaller aid package or one that is composed of only loans. Not a very attractive offer. However, your second choice, College B, gives you either a bigger package or more of your money in grants. Now you are in a position to ask College A to match the offer of College B.

First, email a letter to College A. Begin by stating that you are extremely excited about being accepted and would very much like to attend the college. Explain that given the financial aid package offered, you may not be able to afford the costs. Justify in real numbers why their offer is not sufficient. This, of course, must be true since the college can see all of your family's finances. Not wanting to spend your money is not a good reason. Not having the money to spend is an excellent reason. There is a big difference between the two.

After you make a case for why you need more financial aid, share the better offer made by College B. Include a copy of the award letter from College B with your letter. Point out to the financial aid officer that given the generous package from College B it makes it hard to turn down. Politely reiterate that you would prefer to attend College A and would like to know if there is anything the financial aid office can do to reassess your aid package.

Throughout the letter you want to be friendly and polite. Remember you are not negotiating for a lower price on a car but asking for a reassessment and providing another college's better offer (as well as your own family's finances) as a basis. You want to avoid sounding confrontational or argumentative. You also need to have concrete reasons why you need more financial aid.

This technique does not guarantee success. In fact, no college is under any obligation to change its original offer. However, if you can present a compelling case, you may find that the college is willing to reassess the initial offer and adjust the aid package. You only want to do this with the college you really want to attend. Don't try to pit a whole bunch of colleges against each other. It will only backfire. Focus on your first choice college, and try to use the better offer of your second choice as leverage. If it doesn't work, you can always attend your second-choice college, which offered you the better package.

Get Your Employer to Pay

Get Your Employer To Pay

In the Charles Dickens classic "Great Expectations," we meet a poor boy, Pip, who through an unknown benefactor is sent to London, all expenses paid, to learn to become a gentleman. Most of us would love to have a wealthy benefactor who generously pays for our education. But while few of us will find the kind of benefactor in Dickens' classic, most us do have someone in our lives who may be willing to help: our employer.

Before you assume that your boss would never spring for your tuition, ask yourself one question: Have you asked? If you haven't asked then you don't really know if this is a possibility. Many adults have been surprised at how generous their employers have been when they approached them for help to go back to school. The trick is to approach your boss in the right way and to make sure your going back to school benefits both you and your boss.

In this chapter we'll go over some strategies to help you convince your employer that it is in the company's best interest to help you go back

to school. We'll also let you in on a little secret: many companies already have established programs to pay for employee's tuition expenses. Like year-end bonuses, dental plans and free coffee, education benefits are a fairly common perk at many medium- to large-size companies. Often these benefits are not widely publicized since few employees actually take advantage of them. Therefore, you may already be working for a company that is willing to help you earn your degree and all you need to do is ask.

Alan's Story

When Alan Bovill was offered a new job he didn't think about asking for more money. Although Alan had already earned his undergraduate degree in accounting from Northern Illinois University he wanted to get a master's of business administration. Changing jobs offered him the opportunity to do so and on his new employer's dime. Before signing on to the new job Alan negotiated with his employer for a 100 percent tuition reimbursement.

For the past four and a half years Alan has not only been working full-time but also working toward a graduate degree in international business and finance at the University of Chicago. And every single one of the 17 classes, which cost $3,400 each, has been paid for by his employer.

Alan's program is part-time, which means that instead of taking two years it will take five and instead of two or three classes per quarter he takes one.

While Alan could have taken more classes per quarter he didn't want to abuse his employer's generosity. "If I went hog wild taking classes that would be a lot of money for the company and it might become an issue," he says.

There was an unspoken understanding of the fairness of the deal between Alan and his employer. For Alan to complete his education for free he needs to put in at least five years of work. His employer would not want him to load up on classes, graduate in two years and then change jobs leaving the company holding the bill.

Alan also admits that since his employer was willing to pay for his education, he was more motivated to stick with his program despite the added stress it created. He says, "Since my company was paying for my classes I felt that if I didn't finish the program I was giving up a huge opportunity."

Even with the company paying for it, going to school while working was not easy for Alan, who has a wife and four children. "It is definitely a time commitment," he says. "It is just one more thing to balance between work and home." Homework can be especially disruptive. On exam days Alan does the same thing he did while an undergraduate: he crams. He says that he doesn't do a lot during the quarter. On the day of finals or mid-terms, he leaves work early to cram for three or four hours, which usually results in B's in his classes.

Alan also tries to target classes that will fit into his lifestyle with work and family. He selects classes that don't have a lot of group projects because he knows that he has to travel a lot for work. He usually signs up for two or three classes, attends them for the first week and then decides which one fits best into his schedule. Shopping classes before committing to them gives Alan the flexibility to fit his life, work and family into his education.

Alan's other major obstacle is Chicago traffic. On a good day, his commute is 50 minutes door to door. On average it takes about one hour and 20 minutes and can extend longer when there are Monday night football games in town. He is glad, however, that his commute is not as bad as a few of his fellow students, who fly in from New York, Iowa and Indiana for weekend classes. "Now that's dedication," says Alan.

As for Alan's plans for the future after he receives his graduate degree, he says, "My degree has already helped me in certain aspects of my job. I think nowadays if you are an executive, people really look for a higher level of education. You have a lot of good people that are out in the marketplace looking for jobs so the competition is tougher."

Alan thoroughly enjoys graduate school and is glad he has been given this opportunity. He believes he has certainly made the right choice in order to get ahead of the curve in the job market both now and in the future.

Why Would My Company Pay For My Education?

There are many reasons why a company would want to help you pay for your education. The obvious reason is if your education helps you do a better job. By paying for a computer course, for example, your employer knows that you'll be able to use these newly learned skills to improve your daily work and therefore become a more productive employee.

Another reason a company would be willing to pay for your education is that it is a benefit for recruiting better workers. If you are choosing between two similar jobs but one offers to pay for any career development classes that you take while employed, you will probably accept their job offer.

And a third reason why a company would offer to help pay for your education is in order to keep you. Since you only get these benefits as an employee you must continue to work for the company while you are also getting your schooling. Some companies may even make you sign an agreement to work for them for a certain number of years in order to get your education benefits. It's a trade. The company agrees to pay for your education, and you agree to work for them for a certain amount of time.

What Do These Education Benefits Look Like?

There is no standard education benefit, and companies are free to create whatever they feel is most useful to their employees as well as affordable for their bottom lines. In general, you will find that education benefits fit into one of the following categories:

336.

Tuition assistance

The most common program that your employer will offer is tuition assistance or reimbursement. Companies are free to set their own policies on how these programs work. Some will pay for a certain percentage of your tuition while others will pay up to a specific dollar amount. Most tuition-assistance programs have a grade requirement, which means that if you earn lower than a "B" or "C" your company is not obligated to pay.

The requirement that gives employees the most trouble is that companies usually will pay only for courses that are deemed "work-related." Fortunately, "work-related" is a broad definition that is open for interpretation. You can often make a convincing case for courses that are not related directly to the job that you are doing now but that will help you develop professionally and learn new skills to advance in your career. Take a look at the people who are above you and see what skills and educational backgrounds they have. It makes perfect sense for you to take courses to learn those same skills so that you may be promoted to those positions in the future.

It's important that you talk to your human resources or personnel department and understand all of the rules to qualify for tuition assistance at your company. While many companies have tuition assistance, it is not always widely publicized. We've heard of more than one instance where an adult student spoke to their HR department only to be told they didn't have tuition assistance. Yet, when they asked their direct manager they found out that there was a program but it was run through their department manager and not HR. So be sure to inquire with both your HR department and your department manager.

Finally, be aware that some companies will withhold paying your benefits for up to a year to make sure that you stay at your job. If you quit within a certain period after completing your courses they may deduct what they have paid from your last paycheck. So don't think about taking advantage of tuition assistance if you plan on jumping ship soon.

Here are a few examples of some companies' tuition-assistance programs:

Seagate, the disk drive maker, offers all of its regular employees who have been with the company for at least six months tuition assistance for career-related education. Seagate pays 100 percent of the cost for tuition and required fees and 50 percent of the cost of textbooks, up to a maximum of $7,500 per year. To receive reimbursement, you must achieve a grade of "C" or better in your courses.

If you are an employee of Fairfax County in Virginia, you are eligible for tuition assistance for courses related to your career or to a function of County government. You must also earn a passing grade. The County also offers special Language Tuition Assistance to employees who successfully complete foreign language programs. Both programs reimburse one course per term up to a maximum of three terms per year. Applications are taken on a first come, first served basis.

If you are a manager at a McDonald's you can get reimbursed for 90 percent of eligible expenses, up to a maximum of $5,250 a year ($2,000 a year for part-time employees). If you work for Macy's Department Stores you can get assistance with continuing education on the undergraduate, graduate and MBA level.

Finally, one nice tax benefit of tuition assistance is that anything you receive up to $5,250 per year (as long as it pays for qualified tuition expenses) is not treated as taxable income.

337.

Tuition discounts

Your company may have a deal with schools in your area to give you discounts on certain classes or programs. For example, you may be able to take a computer training class for free or at a steep discount. Or, if you work for a college or university (even if you are a part-time employee) you may receive significant discounts on courses. Many colleges even allow their employees to get a complete education for free.

338.

Free professional development classes

These classes are scheduled by your company and are usually held on site or at a local school. They often cover material that is directly related to your job function. For example, if you work in sales you may be able to attend a training course on negotiation skills.

Many adults find that these free training classes are not mentioned in their company's written employee policy. However, when they inquire with their managers they learn that they can take up to several thousand dollars worth of training classes. Usually your department manager is allocated a set budget at the beginning of the year for employee education. Since this budget changes with the fortunes of the company it is not something that can be guaranteed to every employee. Your manager usually has discretion over these funds and gives them on a first come, first served basis. Ask your manager what kind of training money is available—and be sure to have an idea of what classes you want to take if funds are available.

339.

Employer scholarships

While we covered scholarships from businesses in Chapter 2, it is worth mentioning again that many companies offer scholarships with no strings attached simply because you are an employee. These are great scholarships to win since you are competing against so few other people. Often the only requirement is that you be an employee. Even if you work part-time you may find that this makes you eligible to win an employee scholarship.

340.

Whatever you can negotiate

Sometimes you just need to be creative and convince your boss that helping you further your education is not just a good deed but is also good business. This is especially true if your employer does not already have a program in place.

The key to successfully negotiating education benefits from your employer is to address the following four concerns that your boss has about giving you free money. If you can present a strong and convincing case in each of these areas then the chances are good that your boss will agree to provide you with some valuable education benefits.

What is the benefit to the company of you furthering your education? This is the number one concern of your employer. Every boss needs to justify how investing in your education will profit the company. If your education ties in directly with your current job and will help you to do your work better then the benefit is clear. However, if you want to get an education in a different field then you need to find a way to make the connection to improved job performance. Maybe the skills you'll learn will help you progress up the ranks within the company. Maybe they will help you become a better manager or executive. You need to tie in the knowledge you will receive to how it will help you be a better employee. The one exception is if you are thinking of changing careers and applying for a new job. When you are offered a position, you may negotiate education benefits with your new employer before you start.

What is the cost? No matter how much your education will help you do a better job, there is always going to be limits to the cost. Your boss probably has a budget for the year and will need to take out the money from this budget to pay for your education benefits. You need to make sure whatever you are proposing is reasonable in terms of cost. This might mean you compromise and take fewer classes per semester in order to lower the cost for your employer.

Will you still be an effective worker while you are a student? No manager will agree to pay for your education if it means you won't be able to continue to do an excellent job as an employee. Your manager may fear that you'll start coming in late and missing deadlines because of your new responsibilities as a student. Address these concerns up front. Show your manager how much time being a student will entail and where that time will come from—which should be from your own recreational and personal time. Reassure your boss that your job performance will not be sacrificed and even offer that should your work decline you'll agree to quit school.

Will you stay after you graduate? The last concern your boss may have is whether or not you'll stay after you get your degree. If an employer feels that you are just using them to get a free education and will jump ship after you are done they won't be willing to support you. You may offer to sign a contract to remain with the company for a minimum of one or two years after you graduate. The specific length, of course, depends on the kind of education benefits they provide. Don't be too anxious to make this kind of commitment since you don't want to lock yourself into an agreement that you can't keep or that will make you totally miserable.

When you speak to your boss about education benefits it may be helpful to have everything written out. Eventually, you'll probably sign some type of contract that outlines the responsibilities of both you and your employer. It's important that you are able to speak frankly to you employer about each of these issues and make sure there are no misunderstandings or hidden concerns.

If you make a good case by addressing each of the above areas you'll have a good chance of convincing your employer that it makes good business sense to help you further your education.

Take Advantage of Retraining Programs

Take Advantage Of Retraining Programs

Losing your job or being downsized is unfortunately an all-too-common experience in today's economy. Many adults, however, are taking this otherwise bleak event and turning it into an opportunity by going back to school, gaining new skills and finding better paying jobs. Both the state and federal governments have programs that can actually help pay for this retraining.

You don't always have to be laid off to take advantage of some of these programs. Some also target homemakers who decide to go back to work but realize that they need to get more education to be competitive in the job market. Also, workers who simply decide

that their current jobs won't lead anywhere and want to invest in their education so that they can switch careers or advance to better jobs in the future may qualify for assistance.

Your biggest challenge is to find and decipher all of the various state and federal programs. Also, each program has its own qualifications. In this chapter we will give you an overview of the various programs that are available to help you figure out which ones to pursue and some of the most important agencies that can help.

Dawn's Story

For most people getting laid off from work is a huge emotional and financial tragedy. Or so it was for Dawn Garcia, 47, until she realized that this was the chance she had been waiting for all her life.

"I was never happy with my job, but I wouldn't in a million years have had the courage to quit on my own. I felt that I had too many responsibilities. But getting laid off meant that the decision was made for me. I was forced to make a change," explains Dawn.

Instead of pounding the pavement for another low paying job that didn't give any personal satisfaction, Dawn did what she always dreamed: she went back to school.

Money was her main obstacle. Without a job and bills to pay she needed some help.

"I found the One Stop Career Center by accident. A friend of mine had mentioned that I should visit the center to help me find a job. I didn't want a job but was worried that I didn't have a choice since I couldn't afford school by myself," recalls Dawn. A One Stop Career Center is a clearinghouse for information and programs offered by the state and federal governments.

But at her center she met a counselor who told her about various programs that could help her retrain for a new career.

"I found that I could get grants for learning skills such as computers. I had never used a computer but knew from my nieces and nephews that everyone at school used one," she says.

Dawn also learned from the counselor that her state offered a variety of programs to help displaced workers.

"I was able to use my state's workforce program to get help with my basic education classes. These were courses that I needed to graduate," says Dawn.

While these programs covered only a portion of her tuition expenses they were just what Dawn needed to make going back to school possible. In addition, she tapped her savings, financial aid and applied for a few scholarships.

Now in her last year of her B.A. program with a double major in art and advertising, Dawn is excited with the new possibilities her education will give her. As she reflects on the past few years she concludes, "The funny thing is that if I didn't get laid off I would still be working at my low-paying and joyless job. While it was traumatic to receive that pink slip, looking back it was the best thing that could happen for me and my future."

Federal And State Retraining Programs

From the Federal government there are several programs that you can take advantage of, particularly if you have been laid off or downsized. On the state level you will find a much wider variety of resources that are open to more than recently displaced workers. Often the state will work with a network of charities, foundations, adult education centers and vocational and university systems to create a wide selection of services. Some of these services may be free while others are heavily discounted as long as you qualify for the program.

Here are some places to start:

341. Drop by your One Stop Career Center
Your first step if you get laid off is to visit your local One Stop Career Center. These centers act as clearinghouses for information and programs offered by both the state and federal government. Some of the training services that you can find at a One Stop Career Center include:

- Occupational skills training
- On-the-job training
- Skills improvement
- GED preparation
- English as a Second Language (ESL)
- Math and reading training

You can find a directory of all of the One Stop Career Centers at: http://www.servicelocator.org. You can also call, toll-free, 1-877-US-2JOBS.

342. Department of Labor Adult Training Programs

Most adult training programs are authorized by the Workforce Investment Act. This federal program aims to increase occupational skills, improve the quality of the workforce, reduce welfare dependency and enhance the productivity and competitiveness of the nation's economy. Most services are provided through One Stop Career Centers and include both occupational training and training in basic skills. There are also supportive services including assistance with transportation and childcare to enable an individual to participate in the program. Priority for intensive and training services are given to recipients of public assistance and other low-income individuals. In addition to unemployed adults, employed adults may participate if they are in need of services to obtain or retain employment that allows for self-sufficiency. In 2012 there were more than 21 million jobless people who started retraining.

343. Trade Act Programs

Trade Act Programs assist individuals who have become unemployed as a result of increased imports from, or shifts in production to, foreign countries. The goal of the Trade Act Programs is to help trade-affected workers return to suitable employment as quickly as possible.
Website: http://www.doleta.gov/tradeact/

344. Apprenticeship Training Program

This program is designed to improve apprenticeship and provide other training programs that help workers train to become proficient in a specific vocational skill.
Website: http://www.doleta.gov/OA/

345. Welfare-to-Work Program

This program provides a variety of services including job training help for "hard-to-employ" welfare recipients and non-custodial parents to obtain and keep jobs that will lead to self-sufficiency.
Website: http://www.doleta.gov/programs/

346. Senior Community Service Employment Program

This program provides part-time employment training for low-income persons age 55 or over. The program places participants in community and government agencies for training as well as provides other training necessary to enter the workforce.
Website: http://www.doleta.gov/seniors/

347. Educational Opportunity Centers

Educational Opportunity Centers are part of the federally funded TRIO program. There are 139 Educational Opportunity Centers located throughout the country. These centers primarily serve displaced or underemployed workers from families of four with incomes under $36,450. Services that the EOC provide include:

- Information on postsecondary schools
- Career counseling and assessment
- Academic and educational counseling
- Admission information and application assistance
- Financial aid information and application assistance
- Career interest assessment
- College transfer assistance
- Study related workshops
- GED/tutoring referrals
- Community referrals

Unfortunately, there is no national directory of EOCs. The best way to find them is to do an Internet search for "Educational Opportunity Center" along with the name of your state. Often these centers are based out of a college. Once you find an EOC in your state, contact them to find the EOC nearest you.

348. Get more information at the ETA website

Since adult programs funded by the U.S. Department of Labor, Employment and Training Administration (ETA) change each year, check their website to get the latest information on new and existing programs for adults.
Website: http://www.doleta.gov

349. Find your state "workforce" agency

Under various departments or commissions, your state has programs to help displaced workers retrain or acquire new skills. For example, start with the Employment Development Department in California, the Texas Workforce Commission in Texas and Workforce New York in New York.

At the state level you will find all kinds of resources. For example, the South Florida Workforce (SFW) Board has a network of training programs that take advantage of the state's public and private colleges and vocational schools. The board targets occupations that are in high demand and offers training to help workers enter these fields.

To find your state workforce agency, visit the directory maintained by the Department of Labor, Employment and Training Administration. On their website you can click on your state and be directed to your state's workforce program where you can explore your options.
Website: http://www.doleta.gov/usworkforce/onestop/onestopmap.cfm

350. Women Work! The National Network for Women's Employment

This non-profit organization is dedicated to helping women achieve economic self-sufficiency through job readiness, education, training and employment. The Women Work! network includes more than 1,000 education, training and employment programs. Women Work! serves displaced homemakers, single parents and other women in transition. Find a list of the various education and training programs on their website at http://www.womenwork.org.

Earn Credit for Life Experiences

Earn Credit For Life Experiences

While it might seem impossible to put a price on education, colleges have found a way to do so through the "credit" system. Basically, each class is assigned a certain number of credits based on the difficulty level and/or time commitment. Each credit costs a set amount and it takes a specific number of credits to graduate. Therefore, the more credits you take the more money you'll have to pay.

But what if you could earn some credits for free? Not only would it shorten the amount of time that you had to spend in school but it would also save you a bundle of money.

There are several ways that you may be able to earn credits for free. The most common is if you have already taken some college-level courses. With your transcript you may be able to use those courses to count toward your degree. Of course, if you took courses a long time ago in rapidly changing subjects like computer science, the credits may not count, but for the most part, there is no expiration date for undergraduate credits.

Another way you can earn credit is to show the college that specific life experiences and training you have received while working are equivalent to college credit. You may not realize it, but you have amassed

a variety of skills through your life and some of these can be converted into credit that counts toward your degree.

Some colleges even offer ways to earn more credits than normal through accelerated programs. Also, if your college does not charge based on classes but instead has a set fee per semester, if you load up on extra classes you are effectively getting those courses and credits for free. Of course, you'll be working a lot harder too!

Jane's Story

Jane King, 42, returned to college to get her undergraduate degree in psychology. It was a subject that interested her ever since she was 11 years old and discovered that she could trick her younger brother to do what she wanted by using reverse psychology. "I was just amazed that I could get him to sweep the kitchen by pretending that I wanted to do it and that it was so much fun," she recalls.

Unfortunately, when Jane graduated from high school she needed to take a job in a fish cannery to help support her parents who were struggling to raise her five younger siblings. Marriage and a family of her own soon followed. Now several decades later Jane was finally ready to get the degree that had until now eluded her.

"There was no real economic reason for me to go back to school since I wasn't planning on become a psychologist, but I just had this burning desire to learn more about psychology," recalls Jane.

There was also the fact that Jane's own children would be heading off to college in a few years. They were all in high school, which meant she had her days free. While her family was saving for their educations, they still had a few years to go. Once her children started college she knew that they would have no spare money. "It was now or never for me," she says.

Cost conscious, Jane was determined to get her degree as cheaply as possible. "For me, I wanted to focus on the classes that I loved, which were all about psychology and the science of the brain." But to earn her degree she also had to take many general education courses, including a physical education requirement.

The last requirement struck Jane as odd since for years she had been a marathon runner and had even helped to train several friends to run marathons. The physical education requirement meant she would have to sign up for running, tennis or some other sport. She reasoned that she already knew about the basics. She says, "As a marathon runner you learn about the importance of warming up, stretching, strength training, good diet and treating various running injuries. It seemed to me like a waste of time to take a basic PE class."

Jane spoke to her academic advisor, who agreed and informed her that she could get credit for her marathon experience to pass out of the physical education requirement. All she needed to do was document her involvement with running. She wrote a five-page report, giving a brief overview of her marathon running and then explaining how she already knew most of the material covered by the physical education class.

She got a copy of the previous year's curriculum so that she knew what was covered and then showed how she had experience in each of the areas. She explained how the various running injuries she had sustained had taught her about sports injuries and how to avoid them. She showed how much reading she had done in nutrition to prepare her body to run marathons and explained how her running group had lectures from prominent runners and trainers during meetings.

With this document in hand she submitted it to the department and within a few weeks was granted credit for her physical education requirement. Not only did this prevent her from taking a class for which she already knew the material, but it saved her hundreds of dollars for a course that she didn't need. It allowed her to fill that slot with a psychology course that helped her to graduate faster.

"Who would have thought that my running would actually help me get college credit? The best part about it is that I love to run so basically I was being rewarded for all these years of doing something that I truly enjoyed," says Jane joyfully.

Earn College Credit To Graduate Early

351.

Use the College Level Examination Program to skip classes

Your college may let you take CLEP exams to receive college credit. There are currently 2,900 colleges that give credit to students who pass CLEP exams. There are two types of CLEP exams. One is a general subject exam that covers math, English, humanities, natural science and social science and history. The other is a subject exam that covers a specific course. A passing score in this exam will usually give you credit for that specific course. There are currently 30 subject exams.

A CLEP exam costs $80 to take but could save you thousands of dollars in tuition. Plus, you don't want to take a course in an area in which you are already proficient. To learn more about CLEP and read examples from actual exams, visit http://www.collegeboard.com/student/testing/clep/about.html.

352.

Take a DSST exam

Originally designed for the military, the DANTES Subject Standardized Tests (DSST) can now be taken by anyone. More than 80,000 people take the DSST each year to receive college credit. By passing the DSST exam you can earn credit for what you already know and thus save money. Learn more about the tests and find a test center at http://www.getcollegecredit.com.

353.

Earn credit with Excelsior College Examinations

There are 53 undergraduate-level Excelsior College Examinations that are accepted at nearly 900 colleges and universities. If you're in the military, an added bonus is that the undergraduate-level Excelsior College Examinations (as well as the DSST and CLEP exams) are free. You can preview the test material online, get a free study guide and find a testing location at http://www.regents.edu/exams/.

354.

Take the Graduate Record Exam as an undergraduate

While the GRE is usually for graduate school admission, some colleges allow undergraduates to earn credits with GRE scores. Check with your department to see if GRE scores can be used to satisfy specific course requirements. You can learn more about the GRE at http://www.ets.org/gre.

355.

Job Ready Assessment tests can count for credit

There are 75 Job Ready Assessment tests that you can take to get credit in vocational or technical fields. Exams include tests in accounting, computer programming, construction, drafting, plumbing, welding and more. Visit the National Occupational Competency Testing Institute at http://www.nocti.org.

356.

Get college credit for life experience

If you are an adult or even graduate school student you may be able to get college credit for your professional and life experiences. Most schools recognize that you can gain college-level knowledge through your own life experiences. If your experiences are general and not related to a specific course, you might obtain General Studies credit. Or, you may get credit for specific courses if you have had related experiences or training.

In the book *College Degrees By Mail* there are examples of ways that colleges may recognize life experiences. For example:

• Work can demonstrate such skills as typing, filing, inventory control, accounting, computer programming, welding, editing and sales.

• Homemaking can show your proficiency in home maintenance, household planning and budgeting, childcare, meal planning and nutrition and child psychology.

• Volunteer work can show experience with community service, political campaigns, church activities and service organizations.

The first thing you should do is contact your department or admission office to see what experiences qualify and what kind of substantiation you need to provide.

357.

Get credit through a learning portfolio evaluation

In order to judge whether or not you should receive college credit for your experiences or previous studies, colleges want proof. You can provide this with a learning portfolio. In the portfolio you give a self-assessment, detailing the type of learning or training you have received outside of the classroom. Usually you will write a main essay and provide supporting documents. You want to make a case for how this learning is comparable to college-level learning and prove to the college that you possess the knowledge within this field.

A typical portfolio may include:

- Your work history along with any volunteer experiences
- Formal educational experiences and special training
- Specific recognition for your knowledge including any licenses
- Hobbies and interests
- Meaningful life experiences
- Specific knowledge and skills gained

The key is to not make a laundry list of everything that you have done but instead to explain what you have learned and how it applies to your field of study. Be analytical about what you have gained from the experience, and demonstrate that this learning is equivalent to what you would learn in college. Look at the course catalog and match your knowledge to specific courses. You also need to show that you understand the theories behind your knowledge. In other words, just because you can drive a boat does not mean you understand the theory behind hydrodynamics. It will help if you speak to a member of your department to get the specific details on what your portfolio should look like.

358.

Earn credit by credential evaluation

Credit by evaluation is when a college looks at any education or training that you have received outside of a traditional institution and determines if it is equal to a course offered by the college. This can include course work and training while in the military, while working or in schools that are not accredited or in organizations that are not primarily educational institutions. Speak to your department to request credit by evaluation. Most schools use the *National Guide to Educational Credit for Training Programs,* the *Guide to Educational Credit by Examination* and the *Guide to the Evaluation of Educational Experiences in the Armed Services* published by the American Council on Education (http://www.acenet.edu) to determine how your experience is equivalent to college courses.

359.

Earn credit by taking a proficiency or challenge exam

Some colleges let you take a proficiency exam in a specific course to prove that you have the knowledge or experience necessary to pass the exam. It's like passing the final exam of a course without having actually taken the class. Speak to your professor or department head to see if an exam is an option at your school.

360.

Take an accelerated degree program

If you can't increase the amount of money you have, then the only way to decrease your college costs is to lower the price. One way to do this is to finish early. If you can graduate a semester sooner, that's one less semester that you'll have to pay for. Check if your college or the colleges you are applying to offer an accelerated degree program. Look for one that allows you to graduate in three years instead of four. For example, through Mississippi College's Accelerated Degree Program, you can earn 30 or more hours a year toward your major in business administration, accounting or marketing by attending eight-week sessions that meet twice per week. This shaves off time and therefore money from the cost of your degree.
Website: http://www.mc.edu/accelerated/

361.

Graduate early with summer school

Summer school is often used to get a head start on a class or to make up for less than stellar grades. However, another use for summer school is to build credits that will let you graduate early. Summer school courses are shorter since you often meet every day and cheaper. Another advantage is you can take summer classes near your home and even schedule them around your summer work. Check with your college to make sure that the summer course credits will transfer without any problems.

362.

Take the maximum number of credits you can

If your school charges a set price for the semester you might be able to load up on credits by taking more than the recommended number to help you graduate early. The danger is that you overload yourself, and your grades suffer. However, if you can fit in one or two extra classes each semester you could graduate a semester or even a year early.

363.

Combine a B.A. with a master's degree

If you know that you are going to obtain a graduate degree you might be able to shave a year off of your education (and therefore one year's less tuition payment) by combining your undergraduate degree with a graduate degree. This not only saves you money but may also give you an advantage when job seeking because you'll have an advanced degree. For example, you can earn a bachelor's and master's degree in five years at the University at Buffalo (http://www.grad.buffalo.edu), which has more than 30 combined degree programs in areas including accounting, engineering and social work.

Be a Part-Time Student

Working And Studying At The Same Time

What makes going to school so expensive? Besides the price of tuition, it's the fact that to be a student you also have to be unemployed. Aside from part-time work, most students cannot hold a full-time job. With zero income and tuition to pay, it's no wonder that the student life is synonymous with the poor life.

But why can't you work and go to school? The biggest problem is that class time and work time are usually both between 9 and 5. Plus, there is the all important sleep time. Yet this has not stopped millions of students from working and getting their degree. It can take longer to complete your degree if you opt to work and go to school since

you usually take a reduced class load. The upside is that you can still work and earn money to pay for your education.

There are several options for combining work with school. Some students begin with night programs to get their basic courses out of the way, then move to a weekend course and even finish their last year as full-time students. There is no single "correct" way that you can combine work and school and the only rule is to do whatever fits your specific situation.

Jennifer's Story

Jennifer Greenfield returned to school when she was 27 years old. At the time she was a single mother raising two children without any support. "It was impossible to raise a family on the pay of a nursery school teacher's assistant," she says.

At first, Jennifer went to Medical Tech School, but that turned out to be only the beginning. Medical Tech School led her to SUNY Stony Brook College and then CUNY Queens College, where she recently completed her bachelor's degree in sociology. Not stopping there, Jennifer is applying to CUNY Law School to take her education even further.

Before Jennifer returned to school she had been working at both a nursery school and a camp. She was baby-sitting as well, usually from Friday at 5 p.m. until Sunday at 7 p.m. in addition to caring for her two children. She and her children lived in a small attic apartment and barely made ends meet.

After she enrolled in the Medical Tech School she did so well her teacher suggested she go on to a physician assistant program at Stony Brook. Jennifer liked the idea, in part because she wanted to continue her education and also because they offered family housing.

Unfortunately, Jennifer felt she just couldn't juggle everything at once. "I found that I couldn't work full-time, attend classes, do the required volunteer work and see my kids. So I decided not to do the physician assistant program," she explains. She did stay in school, however, changing her major to sociology. With her new major, Jennifer had more time and was able to continue to work. She worked in the on-campus housing office, running the children's programs while parents attended meetings. Jennifer also worked at a neurologist's office and did freelance computer work reviewing computer software for children.

"It is all about managing your time," she says. "Full-time work can fit in with full-time school and even children, but it takes a lot of juggling. I get up very early, go to sleep very late and study most of the night."

Jennifer is now working as a legal assistant in real estate law and as a research assistant for one of her professors in urban studies. The real estate law job has been particularly useful since she is considering pursuing that area in law school.

Jennifer has always been resourceful and able to manage both work and school, but that doesn't mean it has been easy. She wishes there were an easier way to look for scholarships and grants. "I wish it were easier than sitting in the library for hours and hours to look up scholarships. I don't mind spending time working on the scholarships, but what full-time student, let alone full-time worker and parent, has that kind of time?" she asks.

Jennifer has managed to find a few financial shortcuts. For example, she transferred schools to save money on commuting and time that she could be working to earn money. School became her social life and between that, work and her children she says, "I didn't have the time, money or energy for anything else."

The one thing Jennifer is keenly aware of as an adult trying to make a living at the same time she is a student is the sad fact that "single parents are often looked down on, especially those receiving aid from the government." Jennifer believes that many women who could be in school are held back for fear of losing the assistance that they need to support their children.

"I took that risk anyway," she explains. "I borrowed as much as I could while working and sacrificing luxuries in order to get my degree, and I will continue to do so until I finish law school."

Yet these sacrifices pale in comparison to the benefits. Jennifer knows her degree is her steppingstone to a great future. "It is the gift of a successful future," she says. "It is a chance to be a part of society and not be dependent on that society."

Part-Time Options

Let's take a look at some of the options that let you work while still earning your degree.

364.

Night school isn't just to get your high school diploma

You might think of night schools just as high schools where adults can complete their GED. However, night programs have exploded to encompass everything from single skill courses such as learning shorthand or computer skills to getting your entire bachelor's or master's degree.

Colleges with night programs usually offer classes that meet one or two nights a week. You may be able to sign up for as many as four courses per week. Most schools don't offer courses on Friday or the weekend. These programs allow you to continue working while also working toward learning a new skill or degree.

Don't deceive yourself to think this will be easy. Most night students report that life takes on a whole new level of chaos as they juggle family, work, classes and homework. But the flexibility of night programs can't be matched, and they are usually one of the most economical ways for you to get more education without having to quit your job.

365.

Adult education is often a bargain

If you need vocational or technical training or basic educational skills, adult education may be a great choice for you. State and federally funded adult education centers are usually run out of high schools, community centers, community colleges and public universities. Their primary mission is to provide low- or no-cost training for students who need to acquire new skills due to a forced career change.

Most adult education classes can be taken while working, and in fact your employer may even pay for your schooling. Some programs also give discounts to students over the age of 55, and many states designate certain types of classes as eligible for receiving state subsidies, which greatly reduce costs.

To find programs available in your area, start with your state's office of adult education or simply look online for the nearest adult school.

366.

Use your evenings and weekends to get a degree

Professional schools are getting into the action of helping full-time workers get their advanced degree. The UC Berkeley part-time MBA program is a good example. While a traditional MBA requires that you be a full-time student for two years, the part-time program allows you to work full-time and attend either evening or weekend classes. If you choose the evening schedule you'll meet twice a week for three and a half hours per session. If you go the weekend route you'll meet on Saturdays from 9 a.m. to 6 p.m. You take the same courses as full-time business school students and earn the same degree, but since you are meeting for less time it will take you three years to graduate.

Part-time programs are growing in popularity as an advanced degree becomes more of a career essential and as more adult students find that they cannot afford to give up their jobs to go back to school. Since you won't be giving up your day job you'll need to select a program at a school near you. Call your local colleges and ask about their evening or weekend programs.

367.

Extension programs let you work and study

Most colleges offer continuing education or extension programs. These are typically held in the evening and are usually open enrollment, which means that you don't need to go through a selective admission process to get into the program. Best of all you can earn complete degrees and graduate certificates without having to become a full-time student.

The Harvard Extension School, for example, enrolls more than 13,000 students each year. Unlike the college, the Extension School accepts students on an open enrollment basis. Students can take just a few courses to improve their job skills or they can get an entire undergraduate or graduate degree. The school offers more than 550 courses in 50 fields of study. Many of the instructors are the same faculty who teach during the day at Harvard College.

Contact your local colleges to see if they offer extension or continuing education programs. This may be an excellent way for you to get a degree without being a full-time student.

368.

Summer school isn't only for flunkies

You might think summer school is just for the students who flunked algebra, but most colleges offer summer sessions that allow you to take the same classes that are offered during the school year. If you are lucky enough to be in a profession where you get summers off, then this may be the perfect option for you.

Summer courses are usually more intensive since you have less time to cover the same amount of information as during the regular school term. However, summer school is usually cheaper than the same class taken during the regular term, and you learn the same material. Credit that you earn in a summer course can almost always be used toward your degree or transferred later to a full-time program. Contact your local college to get the details on their summer session and see if it's an option for you.

369.

Explore online learning options

Through online courses you can take classes at your convenience. Online courses also offer a much higher degree of interaction and let you get closer to the feeling of being there without actually being there. As an added benefit, they are often cheaper than in-person courses.

Many colleges and universities now offer distance learning courses. Rutgers University School of Business in New Jersey, for example, offers an online management certificate in everything from marketing to information technology. The program combines online animated instruction and seminars with two one-day, in-person sessions.

There are a lot of ways to find an online degree program. Start by looking at local colleges. Even though you can take courses that are offered strictly online, you may want to take a course that occasionally meets in person. If local colleges don't offer what you are looking for, expand your search geographically by searching for "online degree" and the subject area. Be sure to check the accreditation of the institution.

370.

Don't get a degree when a certificate will do

Less expensive than degree programs, certificate programs are offered part-time, in the summer or through adult education programs and do not require you to take as many courses as you would to earn a full-fledged degree. While not as highly regarded as an actual degree, depending on your reasons for going back to school, they might be just what you need and at a fraction of the cost. Certificates generally signify

What things should I look for when selecting a part-time program?

There's more to studying part-time than finding a program and signing up. Save yourself time and agony by choosing the right program the first time around. Here are some factors to consider:

Academics: Does the program offer the coursework that you seek? Who are the instructors? Can you take classes in other departments?

Finances: Does the school offer aid for part-time students? Will your employer support your education?

Career services: What kind of support does the school provide to help you find a job? Will the career services office put you in touch with alumni? What do students do after finishing the program?

Student life: Does the program offer social events so you can get to know the other students? Are you given access to all of the facilities that a full-time student gets? How close is the school to your home and work?

Balancing with family: Does the school offer childcare? Does it offer programs that your children can attend simultaneously?

If you pick your program carefully you'll stand a much higher chance of being able to fit it comfortably into your already busy life.

proficiency in a specific area, which for career advancement may be all you need to jump to the next level or make a career switch.

371.

Combine part-time with full-time study

What's great about being a part-time student is that you can build up credits while still maintaining your job. After you have built up enough credits through summer, night or weekend programs you may find that you want to finish off your degree in one or two years of full-time study. This may be especially useful if you are looking to change jobs anyway.

By combining part-time with full-time study, you fund your part-time education through work and then you use your savings, scholarships and financial aid to pay for your last year or two of full-time education. You will graduate with a degree from a four-year college and have saved yourself many years of tuition payments.

Smart Saving Strategies for College

Saving For College

College is an investment in your future. With few exceptions you are going to have to contribute some amount of your own money to pay for it. While it is always better to get free cash from scholarships and financial aid, the reality is that the more you save the more options you'll have.

Your personal savings is your best ally when it comes to paying for college. Scholarships are still contests with no guarantees that you'll win. Financial aid changes each year depending on the budgets of the government and college. There is also no guarantee, even if you deserve it, that you will receive all of the financial aid that you need to pay for school.

Plus, if you are like most students and need to take out a student loan your savings will multiply in value. For example, let's say that you need to borrow $50,000 to pay for college. At 3.76 percent interest over 10 years (the typical term for a student loan) you would end up paying more than $10,065 in interest. But if you were able to save half of that amount and borrowed only $25,000 you would pay only $5,033 in interest. That means your personal savings just helped you to avoid $5,032 in additional interest payments. For each dollar that you save you not only need to borrow one less dollar but you also save on the interest that you would have to pay.

The bottom line is that your savings is your money. You have total freedom to use it at whichever college you want. Nothing is as flexible as your own money. In this chapter we're going to show you some of the best strategies for building your savings.

Remember that your commitment to saving money should not end once you get into college. As a college student you'll also have some unique ways to save money and keep your expenses low. As you'll probably learn, college students are experts at living cheaply.

Important: Before we begin remember that this information is meant to provide general guidance about your saving options. You should always check with an accountant regarding your individual situation and to make sure that tax laws haven't changed.

Roberta's Story

Roberta Hunt is a single mother of two who will receive her bachelor's degree two months before her 40th birthday. This is no small feat for a woman who has worked and saved while attending school full-time to receive her undergraduate degree in rehabilitation services.

The degree Roberta is working toward in rehabilitation services will build on the foundation and knowledge that she already has from her occupational therapy associate's degree and her work as a certified occupational therapy assistant.

"I decided to return to school to complete a bachelor's degree because there were no job opportunities in the area I lived. Plus through the Workforce Investment Act (WIA) retraining program, I would receive as much money to attend school as I would in a job in the area," she explains.

Roberta says the decision to return to school was not a hard one to make. She also realized that returning to school would give her more control and opportunities for the future of her career.

It's a decision she is glad she made because she has always had a strong desire to learn. "I felt I was at a standstill in my career and I was also at a bit of a disadvantage economically. I was hardly able to support my family and even when I had a good job, I wanted to increase my earning potential," she says.

In Oregon, Roberta had been paid well as an occupational therapy assistant, but when she moved to New Mexico she could not find work. So Roberta began working at a coffee shop to make ends meet, the only work she could find after she relocated.

However, on Christmas she was laid off from this job. Determined to turn a negative into a positive she enrolled in a few college classes while trying to figure out what to do. "Personally it was not too hard to return to school," she explains. "My hours were flexible and I was able to work a bit during the day." Roberta does say it was hard taking night classes because of the daycare situation with her two children. "The downside of being in school as a single mother was that I had my own work to do in the evenings and I was not able to focus exclusively on my kids' needs after I picked them up from school."

Roberta also worked as a private caregiver and had a day of work as an occupational therapy assistant in an elementary school. "I actually really like working while in school," she says. "I felt like I was doing something tangible and useful. I think it's a great complement to being in school."

But even with an income while in school, Roberta needed to save money aggressively. She moved with her two children to a smaller house to decrease the rent. "It was hard since the cramped space was not conducive to working," she explains. She didn't take her family out to eat often, didn't have cable TV and even dropped her longtime habit of going out for an espresso three times a week, all of which saved her about $70 a month in expenses.

Other than working while in school and constantly saving money, Roberta also looked into various scholarships and applied to those appropriate to her situation. She completed all the applications with no outside help and took extra care not to be "over awarded" since she was in the WIA program and they "frowned on" that sort of thing. "It seems if you receive one award it gets in the way of receiving others," she says. "That was a challenge."

Roberta says that she would have liked to have known what her school expenses would have been for the two years while attending so that she could have figured out how to cover her living expenses with grants and scholarships. She admits she has always been a bit nervous about accruing debt and so far has managed not to while going to school. She has been fortunate to receive grant aid and WIA money and be able to work on the side in order to pay for everything. However, she knows this will not be the case if she pursues graduate school.

"I do think it would have been worth it for me to be willing to borrow some money to work on my degree a while ago. It is very hard to manage, and I think it is better to accept a reasonable amount of debt as long as you are pursuing an education that you truly want," she says.

Overall, Roberta believes that returning to school has been useful as a steppingstone to a graduate degree. "Although it is hard at times to be in school," Roberta explains, "it is worth it, and it is certainly easier to do when one is young." She adds, however, "When you are older I think you are more likely to get more out of it."

372.

Don't ever think that it's too late to start saving

Given a choice, it is better to begin saving four years before you start college rather than four months. But don't throw up your hands in despair if you have only a year or less to save. Because things like financial aid and scholarships are unpredictable, whatever you can save now may be just enough to fill a critical gap. Also, every dollar you save could mean one less dollar you have to borrow. This can save you a lot of money in interest payments. When you think about it, each dollar you save is actually worth a lot more if it helps you borrow less. So no matter how soon you have to pay the first tuition bill, start saving money today.

One last benefit to saving early is that you also begin to train your family to live on less. If you have to stop working to go back to school you'll have to make some changes in your lifestyle. If you can learn to live on less now, then these sacrifices won't seem as difficult.

373.

Identify and eliminate the non-essential luxuries

For many people the key to saving money is to cut unnecessary expenses. Here is a great exercise. Record for an entire month how much you spend. Write down every dollar you spend from food, to clothes, to going to the movies. At the end of the month add up what's on your list. Where is your money going? What expenses are non-essential or luxuries? Do you really need that $4 cappuccino when you could make it at home instead? Does your family need to eat out that often? It may seem trivial but we bet you can find more than spare change to save when you carefully examine how your family spends its money.

One family we know noticed that they were spending nearly $300 a month on restaurant and fast food. They switched to eating at home and doing barbecues when they wanted something special and were able to put more than $3,000 a year toward college.

374.

Put off the big purchases, if you can

Instead of buying a new car, push the old one a few more years. Sure a new kitchen would be nice but so would graduating without having to take out a second mortgage. Remember too that big purchases have long-term consequences. The new car will saddle you with higher insurance payments. Remodeling the bathroom may force you to take out a home equity loan. As long as the purchases are not essential (do spend the money to fix a leaky roof), consider putting them off until after you are done paying for your education.

375.

Postpone college for a year to help you save

One common option is to delay your entry into college for a year. You can usually apply, be accepted and then defer for up to a year when you actually start. By doing this you have a guaranteed spot in next year's class and can focus all of your energies on working and saving money. It can also give you a year to relearn some old study skills. Use the time to catch up on reading and skills that will help you in your program. This will not only make your transition to college easier but it will also insure that you'll graduate on time.

If you are planning on taking a year off, we strongly recommend that you still apply to college and then after you are accepted defer admission by a year. You will need to talk to the admission office to make sure this is possible. Knowing that you have a guaranteed spot in college will save you a lot of stress.

376.

Double or triple your savings with an Individual Development Account (IDA)

Individual Development Accounts (IDAs) are designed for low-income workers to quickly save money for school by matching their savings. The idea is that if you are low income and working, the best way for you to improve your status is to build your savings, which can then be used to purchase an asset such as a house, business or education. To help speed this process the Individual Development Account was established and is managed by a network of non-profit organizations. If you qualify for the IDA program you will set up a goal such as saving $2,000 for college. When you reach that goal, the IDA network will match what you saved by a ratio of two, three or even seven times that amount. Matched funds come from financial institutions, foundations, religious congregations and state and local governments.

For example, if you receive a 2:1 match, which is the most common, each time you deposit $10, you will get an additional $20 credited to your goal. When you reach your goal the money is released directly to the college to pay for your tuition. Having your savings matched speeds up the time it takes for you to reach your goal.

IDA programs usually set their own specific participation requirements. In general, you must be within 200 percent of poverty. This works out to $23,760 for an individual or $48,600 for a family of four. (Be sure to check with your participating IDA program since these levels do vary.) IDA participants must also be employed and agree to take financial planning classes sponsored by the non-profit organization.

The hardest part of participating in an IDA program is finding them. Since the network of IDA providers is composed of a hodgepodge of agencies, there is no national directory. You will have to do some digging. Start with all of the foundations and non-profits in your area. Also try contacting the manager at your local banks. Visit the IDA Network website (http://www.idanetwork.org) and click on "IDA Directory" to find the contact information for various IDA programs in your state. This is not an official or even complete listing of organizations, but it will give you an idea of what you are looking for.

Once you find one in your area make sure you understand the participation guidelines. If you qualify you can definitely speed your way to your educational goal.

377.

Grow your money tax-free with the 529 Savings Plan

Given the buzz about the 529 Savings Plan, you'd think it was the best thing to come along since the invention of compound interest in helping you pay for college. While there are some real advantages to 529 Savings Plans, they are not magical solutions.

Like any investment, 529 Savings Plans don't guarantee specific returns but rise and fall with the market. The tax-free benefits, which are really the major benefits of the plan, only apply to the earnings that are generated. This means if you only have a year or two before you enter college you probably won't notice much of a benefit. 529 Savings Plans work best when you have five or more years to save before entering college.

Nevertheless, there are valuable benefits to some 529 Savings Plans, which may still make them a useful option for you. These include getting state tax deductions for your contributions and also estate planning benefits that allow relatives to contribute a significant amount of money to your 529 Savings Plan.

529 Savings Plans are so popular because they allow families to sock away a lot of money tax-free. Contribution limits are much higher than other savings plans with many 529 plans capping the contribution at almost $400,000 per student. Plus, there are no income limits to who can contribute to a 529 Plan, which means that every family member can participate including rich Uncle Leo.

529 Savings Plans are offered by every state and the District of Columbia, and many states offer more than one. You don't have to participate in your own state's plan and are free to sign up for any of the 529 Plans that are out there. However, you should check your state's tax regulations since about half the states allow you to take a state tax deduction on the money you put into a 529 Plan. If you live in one of these states you'll probably find that with these tax savings your state plan will offer you the best deal.

All of the money that you put into your 529 Plan will grow free from federal income tax. Depending on your state the plan may also be free from state taxes as long as you use the money for qualified college educational expenses.

If not, you not only pay the taxes that you would have owed on any gains but also a stiff 10 percent penalty. Fortunately, 529 Plans are very flexible when it comes to changing the beneficiary. You can use the money from your 529 Plan for any member of your family including, of course, yourself.

So what's the downside? The disadvantage of the 529 is that your investments are determined by the plan. In other words, you don't manage which specific stocks your money is invested in. Most 529 Plans have different investment tracks such as conservative, moderate and aggressive. The plans are very much like a mutual fund where you rely on the fund manager to pick the right mix of investments. But unlike stocks or mutual funds, once you've chosen a track for your 529 Plan, you usually can't modify it for a year.

In addition, for you to see the maximum gains you need to have time to let your money grow. 529 Savings Plans were designed with children in mind and are most effective when you save for 10 or more years. So if you are going to college in a year or two you really won't see that much of a gain and your investment choices will be limited by the plan. It's important to remember that while they offer tax incentives, 529 Savings Plans are not a quick fix to your college money needs.

Why You Should Consider Your State's 529 Plan

The main reasons why you might want to consider a 529 Savings Plan for yourself are to take advantage of state tax deductions and special estate planning benefits.

If you live in one of the following states (Alabama, Arizona, Arkansas, Colorado, Connecticut, District of Columbia, Georgia, Idaho, Illinois, Indiana, Iowa, Kansas, Louisiana, Maine, Maryland, Massachusetts, Michigan, Mississippi, Missouri, Montana, Nebraska, New Mexico, New York, North Dakota, Ohio, Oklahoma, Oregon, Pennsylvania, Rhode Island, South Carolina, Utah, Vermont, Virginia, West Virginia and Wisconsin), you may be able to write off the contributions to your 529 Plan. This is a huge benefit that you should consider when examining your state's own 529 Plan. Remember that tax laws can change so check with your state tax office or accountant to verify that you can still deduct contributions.

Make A Super Gift To Your 529 Savings Plan

If a relative has a chunk of cash that they want to give you to help pay for college, they are limited by the current $14,000 annual gift exclusion. This means that if they give more than $14,000 per year they will be subject to gift tax. However, with a 529 Plan they can actually make five years' worth of gifts in one year. So that means that they could give $70,000 if they are single or $140,000 as a couple to you and count it as a gift made over the next five years. You will not incur any gift taxes, and you will have access to this significant sum of money. This may be an excellent way for parents or grandparents to transfer a large part of their estate without incurring additional taxes.

How To Choose A 529 Savings Plan

Since you can participate in any state's 529 Savings Plan regardless of where you live, you have a lot of options. Maybe too many options. When you are considering the merits of each plan focus on these areas before you invest:

Low expense ratio and other fees. Know what all of the fees are before you sign up. Pay particular attention to annual account maintenance fees, transfer fees and commissions. The annual account maintenance fee is a percentage and is also known as the expense ratio. We recommend that you try to find a plan that has an expense ratio that is under 1 percent a year.

State benefits. You may be eligible for significant benefits if you invest in your own state's plan. These benefits may include state tax deductions on contributions and/or earnings and can more than make up for other shortcomings of the plan. A few states even offer matching contributions!

Investment track options. More options are usually better. Look for a plan that gives you a good mix of investment tracks. (Remember you can switch tracks once a year.) You want as much flexibility in your plan as possible.

Ease of changing account beneficiary. Make sure you can change the beneficiary in case you do not need all of the money.

Other less-important considerations include the minimum amount you need to open the account, conveniences such as online transactions and whether or not the plan accepts contributions at any time in the year.

378.

Don't neglect your IRAs

Compared to a good 529 Plan, using an individual retirement account (IRA) is not the best way to save for college since you don't get the tax-free growth. However, there are some benefits that make building your IRA a smart idea.

When it comes to determining financial aid, your retirement accounts are exempt from consideration. (529 Savings Plans count as part of your assets.) In other words, colleges can't touch these retirement accounts when they try to determine how much money you can afford to pay for college. Plus, you can withdraw money from an IRA before you turn 59 ½ and avoid the 10 percent early withdrawal penalty as long as the money is used for college expenses. This applies to any

IRA you own, whether it is a traditional IRA (including a SEP-IRA), a Roth IRA or a SIMPLE IRA. If you want to learn more about these different IRAs take a look at the IRS's Publication 590. Remember that you might have to pay income tax on part of the money that you withdraw, but at least you avoid the huge 10 percent penalty. Speak with your accountant to determine if this is a good strategy for you.

Don't Stop Saving Once You're In College

Once you become a college student, you'll quickly find that your pockets are more often empty than full. So when you do have some pocket change, you want to do everything you can to make it stretch. To save money, you need to get serious about how you spend your money. This begins by being honest with yourself about how you spend. Take one of your spiral bound notebooks and write in a big, fat marker on the front "Monthly Budget." Track all of your expenses for the entire month. Every dime should be accounted for in this notebook. After the first month review your expenses and figure out how much you spent on necessities versus non-essential items. Most students are surprised to see what they actually spend their money on.

You need to have an accurate idea of where your money is going before you can implement any savings strategies. Once you have identified your weaknesses in spending, you can work to address them by finding cheaper alternatives.

As you begin to save, continue to keep track of your budget until you are confident that you are in control and meeting your monthly savings goals. If you ever find yourself falling back into bad habits, re-open the notebook and start recording your expenses again.

Once you have your budget, you'll find many ways to save. Here are a few ideas to get started:

379. Put yourself on the envelope budget
One highly effective way to control your spending is to use what is called the envelope budget. Get several envelopes and label them with the main categories of your monthly budget. For example you might have "food," "entertainment" and "basic living" envelopes. Put in the money that you have allotted for each activity based on your

monthly budget. During the month take money
from the appropriate envelope, but once your
envelope is empty, stop buying. If you run out
of your entertainment funds mid-month, you'd
better start looking for some free options to have
fun. This trains you to pace your spending
and to live within your monthly budget.
You can even carry any extra money
over so that you can save for something special such as a spring break
vacation.

380. Use your credit cards responsibly

While credit cards are virtually a necessity in our society, they can
also lead to a lot of trouble if used irresponsibly. Anyone with a credit
card can be tempted to spend indiscriminately, but putting it on the
plastic means you have to face the consequences 30 days later when
the bill is due. If you don't pay your balances in full at the end of each
month, you subject yourself to interest payments and late fees that can
potentially destroy your budget.

For example, let's say you made a $2,000 purchase and only paid the
monthly minimum (about 2 percent) each month. On a card with an
18 percent APR, it would take you 19 years to pay off the purchase,
and your total cost would be more than $5,800! Credit cards require
a lot of self-restraint to be used responsibly.

381. Cash is king

Credit cards are great, but you risk spending beyond your means and
paying exorbitantly high interest rates. Avoid the trouble altogether
by paying for everything in cash or (preferably non-bouncing) check.
One student who got into trouble with his credit cards instituted a 100
percent cash system. He discovered that he became acutely aware of
how small impulse purchases could drain his stash. In fact, he became
so cost conscious that he ended up saving money each month. By the
end of the year he had a pile of extra cash in the bank.

382. Swap your credit card for a debit card

If you simply can't control your credit card spending but don't want to
give up the convenience of paying by plastic then consider changing
your credit card to a debit card. A debit card offers all of the conve-

nience of a credit card except that the money is deducted from your bank account when you use it. This way you are not able to spend more than you have.

383. Save your pennies
Remember the penny jar you had as a child? There is no reason you can't do it now as an adult. Find a jar, cut a small slit in the cover and tape it shut. Every time you have change in your pocket, drop it into the jar. At the end of the semester you'll be surprised at how much you've accumulated. Better yet roll those pennies into a bank account that pays interest and let your coins grow.

384. Never buy a textbook
How often does this happen? On the first day of class your professor hands out a reading list of books. You spend a small fortune and a considerable amount of time to buy these books. But as the semester progresses, you realize you only read a few chapters in each book–or maybe you never get around to reading the assignment at all.

Rather than buy new or even used books that you'll only read a small portion of, use the library's copies or borrow them from your class-mates. Professors seldom assign entire books to read. Through some strategic borrowing you should be able to complete all the assignments without buying a single book.

Some of the better sources for used textbooks (don't forget your local used bookstore) include:

- http://www.amazon.com
- http://www.efollett.com
- http://www.barnesandnoble.com/textbooks/
- http://www.chegg.com

385. Shop like a senior–senior citizen that is
Senior citizens who are on a fixed income rarely shop without that valuable money saver: coupons. But if you think poring over the Sunday paper with a pair of scissors is too much work, you can find coupons with a click of your mouse. Online coupons are much easier to find and use. Here are a few sites:

- http://www.mycoupons.com
- http://www.fatwallet.com

- http://www.thecouponclippers.com
- http://www.dealzconnection.com
- http://www.currentcodes.com
- http://www.retailmenot.com

386. Cut your cell phone bill

Heading off to college is a good time to re-evaluate your cell phone plan. The one thing you want to test before buying a cell phone is whether or not you have reception on campus. Some providers are better than others on campus so you might want to wait until you get to college before picking a cell phone service. Once you figure out which services are strong on campus, shop around to find the best plan. Many carriers have unlimited plans, especially for families. Your college may also offer a student discount on cell phone plans.

387. Start packing your own lunch

Instead of buying the overpriced pizza at the student center, why not pack your lunch? Sure it's less convenient, but brown bagging it is easy on the budget. If you have kids that you send off to school each morning then all you need to do is pack an extra lunch for yourself. For some ideas on cheap and easy recipes take a look at *Recipes and Tips for Healthy, Thrifty Meals* that is available for free at http://www.pueblo.gsa.gov.

388. Get your technology at the bookstore

Schools often have some amazing deals for students on computers and software. Before you buy a computer or software at a retail store, check out the deals at your college bookstore. Often you'll find that you can save a ton of money. The same may also be true for cell phone plans and even gym membership.

389. Take advantage of every free service your school offers

Your college is really a mini-city that offers all kinds of perks. Most schools have fitness centers and pools that you can use for free just by flashing your student ID. Many offer free or low-cost tutoring and remedial education programs, and some even have daycare.

390. Get free food at campus events

You know where the free food is on campus. At campus events! Whether it's an Earth Day celebration or a concert sponsored by one of the campus clubs, there is always free food and drinks. Make it a habit to look for posters and fliers announcing these events to get your free grub.

391. Spare the air by taking public transportation or biking

By going carless, you save money on gas, car insurance and parking. Plus, you help the environment. Check out options for biking and public transportation. If you ride the bus or train, investigate getting a pass.

392. Trim your rent

The easiest way to save on rent short of moving is to get a roommate. Turn an extra room or an extra large apartment into extra cash. Be aware, however, that some apartments have legal occupancy limits and your apartment manager may want to raise the rent. So before you do anything, run it by the manager and see if adding an extra person will save you money.

If you add a roommate, you'll probably have to sign a new lease with both of your names on it. This is important because it will legally obligate your new roommate to pay the rent and for any damages to the apartment. You'll also want to sign the renters' equivalent of a pre-nuptial. Spell out everything that might be the source of a problem later such as who takes out the garbage, the noise level and what the policy is on guests staying over. (Roommates' significant others have been known to bunk rent-free for months at a time.) If things don't work out and you want to part ways with your roommate, you'll have something to back up your claims.

While each state has different laws that protect renters, do some basic research about how adding a roommate will affect you legally. Several good articles including "Are You Ready for a Roommate Quiz" appear on the website at http://www.move.com. You'll also find a database of potential roommates.

393. Live in a co-op

If you're willing to put in a little bit of cleaning, cooking or other household-type work,

you can save money by living in a co-op. For students in Ann Arbor, Michigan, the Inter-Cooperative Council (ICC) has 18 houses and one apartment house in which students pay lower prices for room and board. Prices are lower because the co-ops are owned and run by the student members rather than landlords or the university, and student members contribute a few hours of work per week to take care of cooking, cleaning and other household duties. Check with your college to see if co-ops are available.
Website: http://www.icc.coop

394. Work for your rent
Residents who live near campus may have an extra room or cottage that they are willing to let you live in for free in exchange for doing a certain amount of work, such as housecleaning, yard work, errands and childcare. Visit the housing office at your college to learn what kind of unique work for rent opportunities exist in your area.

395. Avoid student activity fees of all types
Besides tuition and room and board, there are a host of other fees that range from activities fees to athletic coupon books. Avoid every fee that you don't think you'll use, especially if you can pay the fee later if you decide you want the service.

396. Use your or your spouse's health insurance
Most colleges automatically enroll you in their health care plan unless you opt out by showing that you already have insurance. If you or your spouse already has health insurance from work that covers you then you can save some money by opting out of the college insurance plan.

397. Ask for student discounts everywhere
You're a student now and entitled to any discount that you can get. Take advantage of your status. Student discounts are offered by many attractions such as movie theatres, ski lodges and amusement parks. You can also get discount entertainment coupon books from http://www.entertainment.com.

Tax Breaks
for Students

Get Your Tax Dollars Back

The old saying is there is nothing certain in life except death and taxes. If you are going to college you can add one more certainty to your life and that is tuition bills. Fortunately, Uncle Sam acknowledges this reality and offers several valuable tax credits and deductions. These tax breaks literally put money back in your pocket to help you pay those inevitable tuition bills.

The challenge with tax breaks is two-fold. First, you need to decipher the tax codes to determine if you actually qualify for a tax break. Most of the tax breaks have income limits and other requirements that restrict their use. Second, if you qualify to take advantage of multiple tax breaks you need to figure out which combination will give you the most benefit. To complicate matters (and you shouldn't expect anything less from the IRS), some of these tax breaks are mutually exclusive, which means you'll have to choose which one to take.

Before you jump in and take advantage of any tax break, do a little long-term planning and create several scenarios to see how each choice affects your bottom line.

Important: Before we begin remember that this information is meant to provide general guidance. You should always check with an accountant or tax planner regarding your individual situation and to make sure the tax laws haven't changed. You should also get the latest version of IRS publication 970 at http://www.irs.gov. With this caution in mind, let's take a look at some of the tax breaks that you may be able to use.

Paula's Story

Paula Greene always got her taxes done by a discount tax preparation service. Her taxes were straightforward and she felt that it was worth it to pay someone else to fill out all of those confusing forms.

It wasn't until Paula was in her second year of college at the age of 38 that she realized how big of a mistake she had made. "One day I was having lunch with some of the other older students at my school when they started to talk about the American Opportunity tax credit. I had no idea what they were talking about and when I heard that it was a $2,500 credit I just assumed that my tax preparation service had been taking care of it," recalls Paula.

But Paula had a nagging feeling that maybe her tax preparation service was not as thorough as she assumed. So Paula dug out her tax forms and carefully went over them line by line. "It was not easy. I hadn't done my own taxes in years and it took hours to figure out what each line meant. But when I got done I was convinced that they had not taken the tax credit," says Paula.

Making a few calls to her friends, Paula became sure that her tax preparation service had goofed. She made an appointment with her service the next day and after going over the documents the representative agreed. Paula was due the $2,500 credit.

"I was kind of upset," recalls Paula, "Here I was struggling to pay for tuition and saving every penny and with one simple mistake they had given away $2,500. That was a huge amount of money for me."

Fortunately, the tax service agreed to file an amended return so that Paula could claim her credit. "It still makes me cringe at how close I came to losing that money. The worst part is if it wasn't for the chance conversation with friends over lunch I would never have even known about it."

Paula is now much more diligent with her taxes. While she still uses a preparation service, although not the same one that made the mistake, she makes sure she goes over each line of the return. She also reminds her tax preparer each year that she is a full-time student so that she won't miss any more tax breaks.

The No Double-Dipping Rule

One important function of tax breaks is that they are designed to refund you money that you have paid out of your pocket for college expenses. To claim a tax credit you therefore must have spent your own money on your education. That money can't come from a source that is already tax-free such as scholarships, veteran educational assistance, Pell grants or 529 Savings Plans. This is because any money that already receives favorable tax treatment cannot be claimed for an additional tax credit. Doing so is known as "double dipping," which is a big no-no to the IRS.

398.

Give yourself up to $2,500 with the American Opportunity tax credit

This tax credit reduces your taxes dollar for dollar and is like putting money directly into your pocket. You may receive up to $2,500 in American Opportunity tax credits if you are in an undergraduate degree or certificate program. (Unfortunately, graduate and professional programs are excluded from this tax credit.)

To figure out how much of an American Opportunity tax credit that you can claim, look at the total amount of money that you paid out of your own pocket for tuition. The American Opportunity tax credit can only be used for tuition and related expenses such as for required books and supplies, not room and board and other expenses. Once you know how much you've paid out of pocket for tuition, you can claim 100 percent of the first $2,000 and 25 percent of the next $2,000 that you paid. In other words to claim the full $2,500 you must have paid at least $4,000 in qualified education expenses.

To claim the American Opportunity tax credit you must also meet the income requirements. For a single taxpayer you can get the full credit if your modified gross adjusted income does not exceed $80,000. If it does but is below $90,000 you can claim a partial credit. For married couples filing jointly you can get the full credit if your income does not exceed $160,000. If you earn more but are still below $180,000 you can claim a partial credit.

To claim an American Opportunity tax credit, file your taxes using Form 1040 or 1040A and attach Form 8863 Education Credits. There are a few other stipulations attached to the American opportunity tax credit, which are that you must be enrolled at least half-time, be enrolled in a program that leads to a degree, certificate or other recognized educational credential and be free of any felony conviction for possessing or distributing a controlled substance.

399.

If you're over the income limit you may get a partial credit

Like all tax credits, the American Opportunity tax credit has an income requirement. If you are over the initial limit, which is $80,000 for single filers and $160,000 for joint filers, but still below the maximum limit, which is $90,000 for single filers and $180,000 for joint filers, you can claim a partial credit.

To figure out how much you can claim, take the amount that you are over the limit and divide it by the phase-out range. This tells you by what percentage you are over the initial limit. You can then take the remaining percentage (the percentage by which you are still under the maximum limit) and multiply it again by the American Opportunity credit of $2,500 to figure out how much you can claim.

For example, if you are a single filer and you earn $83,000, you are $3,000 over the initial limit of $80,000. You divide that $3,000 by the phase-out range, which is $10,000. The phase-out range is simply the difference between the maximum limit of $90,000 and the initial limit of $80,000. This gives you 0.3, which means you are 30 percent over the initial limit. You can therefore still claim up to 70 percent of the credit or up to $1,750 ($2,500 maximum credit x 0.7 = $1,750.)

The process is the same for joint filers only now the phase-out range is $20,000 since you take the difference between $160,000 and $180,000.

400.

Get up to $2,000 with the Lifetime Learning credit

The Lifetime Learning credit is similar to the American Opportunity credit and reduces the tax you owe dollar for dollar. But unlike the American Opportunity, the Lifetime Learning credit can be used for college expenses beyond four years, graduate school or even continuing education. However, you cannot claim both an American Opportunity and a Lifetime Learning credit in the same year. It is usually to your advantage to claim the American Opportunity tax credit if you're eligible and if not, to claim the Lifetime Learning credit.

If you are an adult student who has already completed four years of undergraduate work, are enrolled less than half-time, are taking continuing education courses or if you are a graduate school student, then you have no choice but to take the Lifetime Learning credit.

The maximum amount of the Lifetime Learning credit is $2,000 per tax return, which is figured out by taking 20 percent of what you

pay for tuition (not room and board or other expenses) up to $10,000. This means that to claim the full $2,000 credit, you must spend $10,000 or more out of your own pocket on tuition. Remember, money that is already receiving a tax benefit like scholarships that are tax-free or 529 Savings Plan money doesn't count in figuring out how much you spent. The IRS doesn't allow double-dipping.

Like the Lifetime Learning credit, there are income limits to qualify. For a single taxpayer you can get the full credit if your modified gross adjusted income does not exceed $55,000. If it does but is below $65,000 you can claim a partial credit. For married couples filing jointly you can get the full credit if your income does not exceed $110,000. If you earn more but are still below $130,000 you can claim a partial credit.

Eligible courses can be part of a postsecondary degree program or taken to acquire or improve job skills. Eligible educational institutions include any college, university, vocational school or other postsecondary educational institution eligible to participate in a student aid program administered by the Department of Education. This includes virtually all accredited, private or public, nonprofit and proprietary (privately owned, profit-making) postsecondary institutions. Also, the felony drug conviction rule that might prevent you from getting an American Opportunity credit does not apply for the Lifetime Learning credit.

401.

Choose your tax credit wisely since you can only claim one per year

You can claim only one tax credit per year, which means you need to decide whether to claim the American Opportunity or Lifetime Learning credit if you qualify for both. Here is a handy comparison between the Lifetime and American Opportunity credits:

Lifetime Learning credit

- Up to $2,000 credit per return if you spent $10,000 or more of your own money on qualified tuition expenses. The amount that you can claim is less if you spent less. To figure the credit, take 20 percent of what you spent on qualified expenses up to the maximum of $10,000.
- You can claim a Lifetime Learning credit form postsecondary education (including adult education) beyond four years, for courses to acquire or improve job skills and for studies in which you are enrolled less than half-time.
- You do not need to be pursuing a degree or other recognized educational credential.

- The felony drug conviction rule does not apply for the Lifetime Learning credit.

American Opportunity credit

- Up to $2,500 credit per eligible student. To get the maximum amount you must have spent at least $4,000 on qualified tuition expenses.
- The American Opportunity credit is available ONLY for the first four years of postsecondary education. If you qualify for both the American Opportunity and Lifetime Learning Credit, you probably want to take the American Opportunity credit.
- You must be pursuing an undergraduate degree or other recognized educational credential.
- You must be enrolled at least half-time for at least one academic period.
- You cannot have any felony drug convictions.

402.

Be sure to get your tax credits in the right order

Since you can claim only one of the credits per year, make sure you take advantage of them in the right order. If you qualify for both then you probably want to use the American Opportunity credit. The American Opportunity credit lets you qualify for the full amount while using less of your own money.

403.

Lower your income to claim a tax credit

If you are over the income limits that trigger a phase-out for any tax break, you may be able to change your modified gross adjusted income just enough to qualify for the full credit or a larger partial credit. The key is to boost your contributions to your 401k, 403b or 457 retirement plans. Since this money is deducted before you get your paycheck, in the eyes of the IRS you never see this money. The same is true for any flexible spending accounts for medical or daycare costs that you have. By increasing your contributions to these accounts you will lower your adjusted gross income. This might be enough to give you a bigger slice of the tax break pie. Plus, money in your retirement accounts is sheltered from the financial aid calculations, which can increase your chances of getting more financial aid from the college.

404.

Deduct your tuition and fees

Tax deductions are not as good as tax credits but they do reduce your taxable income, which means you will still pay less taxes. One of the most common education deductions is for money that you pay for tuition and fees. This can be the tuition that you paid either for yourself, a spouse or a dependent child. You can deduct up to $4,000 of tuition expenses (not room and board or other expenses) that you paid as long as you are not also claiming an American Opportunity or Lifetime Learning credit. This is part of the no double-dipping rule, which also means that you cannot deduct any tuition expenses that you paid with tax-free money such as funds from scholarships or 529 Savings Plans.

To claim the full deduction you must also meet income requirements. If you are a single taxpayer with a modified adjusted gross income of $65,000 or less or a couple filing jointly with an adjusted gross income of $130,000 or less you can take the full deduction. If you make more

---

What's the difference between a tax credit and a tax deduction?

Tax credits reduce the amount of tax you owe dollar for dollar. Therefore, a tax credit of $1,000 means you will pay $1,000 less in taxes. A tax deduction reduces the amount of money on which your tax is calculated. A tax deduction of $1,000 may save you $200 in taxes depending on your tax bracket.

but still less than $80,000 as a single taxpayer or $160,000 as a joint taxpayer you can deduct only up to $2,000 in tuition expenses.

405.

Don't forget you can deduct your student loan interest

All student loan interest that you pay is tax deductible up to $2,500 per year. The loan must have been used for qualified higher-education expenses, including tuition, fees, room and board, supplies and other related expenses. Also the maximum allowable deduction is gradually reduced for single taxpayers whose modified adjusted gross income exceeds $65,000 but is below $80,000 and for married taxpayers filing jointly whose modified adjusted gross income exceeds $130,000 but is below $160,000.

You can usually count as interest the loan-origination fees (other than fees for services), capitalized interest, interest on revolving lines of credit and interest on refinanced student loans, which include both consolidated loans and collapsed loans. You can also count any voluntary interest payments that you make. To claim the deduction you should receive form 1098-E from your lender or loan servicer.

406.

Educational benefits from your employer may be tax-free

If you have a generous employer you might be able to receive up to $5,250 of tax-free employer-provided educational assistance benefits each year. This means that you may not have to pay tax on amounts your employer pays for your education including payments for tuition, fees and similar expenses, books, supplies and equipment. This can be used for both undergraduate and graduate-level courses. Plus, the payments do not have to be for work-related courses. However, you cannot use any of the tax-free education expenses paid for by your

> **How do I calculate my modified adjusted gross income (MAGI) to see if I can deduct what I paid for tuition and fees?**
>
> For most taxpayers, your modified adjusted gross income is simply your adjusted gross income (AGI) on your tax return. If you file Form 1040A, your MAGI is the AGI on line 21 without taking into account any amount on line 19 (tuition and fees deduction). If you file Form 1040, your MAGI is the AGI on line 37 without taking into account any amount on lines 34 or 35 (tuition and fees deduction or domestic production activities deduction.) You must add back to your income any foreign earned income exclusion, foreign housing exclusion, foreign housing deduction and the exclusion of income from American Samoa or Puerto Rico.

employer as the basis for any other deduction or credit, including the American Opportunity and Lifetime Learning credits.

407.

Cash in your government bonds tax-free

If you cashed in a government savings bond to pay for qualified educational expenses you may be able to exclude the interest earned from your federal incomes taxes. The key is that you must have purchased a series EE bond issued after 1990 or the series I bond. The bond must be issued either in your name or in the name of both you and your spouse. You must have been at least 24 years old at the time when you purchased the bond.

If you meet these requirements and the modified adjusted gross income requirement, you can deduct the interest used to pay for tuition. You will need to file form 8815 to figure out your education savings bond interest exclusion.

408.

Money-saving tax benefits of scholarships and fellowships

If you received an academic scholarship or fellowship that is used for qualified tuition, fees and books then it is generally not taxable. For a scholarship or fellowship to be non-taxable you must meet the following conditions:

- You are a candidate for a degree at an educational institution,
- The amounts you receive as a scholarship or fellowship must be used for tuition and fees required for enrollment or attendance at the educational institution, or for books, supplies and equipment required for courses of instruction and
- The amounts received are not a payment for your services.

You cannot exclude from your taxable income any scholarships or grants that are used to pay for room and board.

409.

Get more tax help

Tax questions are never easy, and it is essential that you talk to a professional accountant. In addition, tax laws are constantly changing. To get the latest (and free) information, surf over to the IRS website at http://www.irs.gov or schedule a phone or personal appointment. You can call with questions to 800-829-1040, or try the IRS's Everyday Tax Solutions service by calling your local IRS office to set up an in-person appointment. If you have access to TTY/TDD equipment, call 800-829-4059.

Loan Forgiveness Programs and Scholarships for Service

Have Your Student Loans Forgiven

Under normal circumstances, you can only avoid repaying your student loan if you become disabled or die. We're sure you would much rather pay off your loans than take one of these options. However, there is one other way to have your loan cancelled that does not involve death or bodily injury. This is through what are known as loan forgiveness or loan repayment programs.

Many of these programs are run by state governments as a way to encourage you to enter a specific profession or to work in an underserved area. If you agree to the terms of the program then for each year you meet these obligations the state will pay off a percentage of your loans. Typically after four or five years your loans are completely paid off.

Some state-supported loan repayment programs are reserved only for residents of the state. However, this is not true for all programs. Some allow anyone to participate as long as they work in the state. That means you can go to college in one state, relocate and work in the state with the program and still reap the benefits. Be sure to check both your own state's programs as well as any states where you might consider working.

Closely related to loan forgiveness programs are scholarships for service. These awards are contingent on your obligation to perform a specific duty. This might include studying and working in a specific field. Or it could be doing volunteer work and community service. There are both national and state-based scholarships for service.

The major catch for both loan forgiveness programs and scholarships for service is that both require you to study specific subjects, enter certain occupations or perform certain volunteer duties. If you are willing to meet these requirements then these programs are an excellent way to help cut the cost of your education.

Hee's Story

Hee Ryu found herself a divorced woman in America with two small children, ages 4 and 1, and a job she knew was leading her down a path to nowhere. Some people might have thrown up their hands and given up. After all, Ryu who emigrated from Korea had limited English language and job skills and no family to help.

But at the age of 31 Ryu decided to go back to college and earn not only her associate's degree, which she received from Georgia Perimeter College, but also her bachelor's degree in history from Agnes Scott College. Ryu is now finishing up her law degree from the University of Georgia School of Law.

All of this goes to show what a person can accomplish when she sets her mind to it. "I was scared," Ryu admits. "It was the biggest leap of faith I have ever taken in my life. I had two children to support and I had to let my alteration business go in order for me to attend school full-time."

Ryu first began working at an alteration shop when she moved to the United States years earlier. She says she did not have any job skills. "I could not go out to get a job because I could not afford childcare expenses. I needed to find work I could do at home. I babysat while teaching myself sewing." One year later, Ryu was able to open her own alteration shop, more out of necessity than anything else. "I opened up the alteration shop so that my children could come to the store after school."

Coming to the United States was an entirely new direction for Ryu. When she attended school in Korea all she really wanted from life was a man to marry so she could be a good wife and mother. Living in America made her realize there was so much more.

Ryu had managed to work at odd jobs during her entire education splitting time between tutoring students at her home, serving tables, internships, housekeeping and sewing, just to name a few.

In the beginning Ryu only went to school part-time since she was working and raising two young children. However in the past few years she has been attending school full-time while also managing to make a living and taking advantage of scholarships and financial aid.

"Financial aid itself was not enough to cover all of my expenses. I had to work full-time most of the years I was in school," she explains. "However, without financial aid I don't think I could have made it."

A large part of Ryu's financial aid came in the form of student loans. By the time she graduates with her law degree she will have racked up $110,000 in debt. To pay off this huge sum of money, she turned to a loan repayment program. Working for Atlanta Legal Aid, Ryu was able to qualify for a loan reimbursement plan. The program contributes $500 a month and she pays $75 a month. "Without loan forgiveness I could not pay my bills. I have to pay this loan, probably for the rest of my life," she says.

Ryu says that when it came to researching financial aid information she found many allies. The financial aid officers helped her with the applications, reviewing the forms and answering her questions, and with looking for scholarships. The office had a resource book filled with scholarship information and even application forms.

Ryu says she used the financial aid resource book extensively. A financial aid officer even put a flier for a scholarship in her box, which she eventually won. "Perhaps they went the extra mile for me because I asked for more of their attention," Ryu speculates. But in her view she had little choice. Quitting school was never an option for her and receiving scholarships and financial aid was her only choice. "I had to do it because I did not have any money and, given my responsibilities as a mother and a student, I could not go out to work 40 hours. Therefore scholarships were the only option for me."

Nevertheless, no matter how much money Ryu owes for her education or the trying times she had to endure, she believes that "education is the best investment in life." Her plans when she receives her law degree are to help single mothers struggling to survive with very little financial means. "My divorce process was extremely painful, in part because I did not have a good lawyer."

She says that her job at Atlanta Legal Aid doesn't pay as much as she could make elsewhere, but she appreciates the loan forgiveness program and she also feels her job is helping others. She says she mostly handles family law cases, including divorce and custody, child support enforcement and bankruptcy cases. "It adds an important meaning and purpose to life and I plan to keep it for a long time," she says.

National Loan Repayment And Scholarship For Service Programs

Let's start by taking a look several national programs. Most are designed to encourage you to give a year or two of your life to volunteer work. Many students consider this an invaluable experience. As a reward for giving your time, these programs offer educational benefits that can help you defray the cost of college.

410. AmeriCorps
Run by the Corporation for National and Community Service, AmeriCorps volunteers serve through more than 2,100 non-profits, public agencies and faith-based organizations. Volunteers perform a range

of services including tutoring, building affordable housing, cleaning parks and streams and helping communities respond to disasters. As an AmeriCorps volunteer you will serve either full- or part-time over a 10- to 12-month period.

As a full-time member you may receive $5,815 to pay for college, graduate school or to pay back student loans. You also receive health insurance, training and student loan deferment, and depending on your service even a living allowance. If you volunteer on a part-time basis you receive a partial education award.

You can earn up to two awards, which means that if you serve for two years you can earn more than $11,000 for college or grad school. This goes a long way in helping you pay for college or to cut your student loan payments.

If you are planning to attend school after your AmeriCorps service you may also be able to take advantage of college credit offered by some colleges for your service. For example, the University of Vermont offers both course credit and scholarships for AmeriCorps volunteers. Websites: https://www.nationalservice.gov/programs/americorps and http://www.nationalservice.gov

411. Teach For America
Each year, Teach For America selects 2,000 recent college graduates for training to become full-time, paid teachers in urban and rural public schools. In Teach For America you will receive a salary and health insurance similar to other beginning teachers. You can also qualify to receive forbearance on your student loans and the same AmeriCorps education award of $5,815 for each year of service. You can use the education award to pay back your student loans or toward your future education.
Website: http://www.teachforamerica.org

412. Volunteers In Service To America (VISTA)
If you volunteer 1,700 hours with private, non-profit groups that help eradicate hunger, homelessness, poverty and illiteracy, you may receive $5,815 toward repayment of your student loans, a living allowance and deferment of student loans. As part of AmeriCorps, VISTA focuses on empowering people in low-income areas. As a volunteer you work as a community organizer by doing work such as recruiting

volunteers, fundraising or helping to develop a new program.
Website: http://www.friendsofvista.org

413. NIH Loan Repayment Program

This program provides repayment of up to $35,000 per year of
educational loan debt and federal and state tax reimbursements for
professionals pursuing careers in clinical, pediatric, contraception and
infertility or health disparities research. Among the requirements,
you must conduct research in one of the fields in a project sponsored
by non-profit or government funds for the next two years and have
earned an M.D., Ph.D., Pharm.D., D.O., D.D.S., D.M.D., D.P.M.,
D.C., N.D. or equivalent doctoral degree and be a U.S. citizen or
permanent resident.
Website: http://www.lrp.nih.gov

414. National Health Service Corps

This program pays for tuition, fees, a stipend and supplies for health
professional students who work in underserved areas. Applicants must
be enrolled, or accepted for enrollment, in a fully accredited U.S.
allopathic or osteopathic medical school, family nurse practitioner
program (master's degree in nursing, post-master's or post-baccalaureate certificate), nurse-midwifery program (master's degree in nursing,
post-master's or post-baccalaureate certificate), physician assistant
program (certificate, associate, baccalaureate or master's program)
or dental school. Scholars attending medical school are expected
to complete residency programs in one of the following specialties:
family medicine, general pediatrics, general internal medicine, obstet-
rics/gynecology, psychiatry or rotating internship (D.O.s only) with a
request to complete one of the above specialties. Dental scholars may
do residencies in general practice or pediatric dentistry. Recipients
must also serve full-time, commit to working in an underserved area
for at least two years and be U.S. citizens.
Website: http://nhsc.hrsa.gov

415. Extramural Loan Repayment Program for Clinical Researchers (LRP-CR)

Physicians and scientists may have up to $35,000 of their loans repaid
annually for conducting patient-oriented research. Applicants must be
U.S. citizens or permanent residents; hold an M.D., Ph.D., Pharm. D.,
Psy.D., D.O., D.D.S., D.M.D., D.P.M., D.C., N.D., O.D., D.V.M. or
equivalent degree and have qualifying educational debt.
Website: https://www.lrp.nih.gov

416. Association of American Medical Colleges

There is a directory of loan repayment programs for health-related professionals on the website of the Association of American Medical Colleges in the financial aid section at http://www.aamc.org. In exchange for loan repayment, medical professionals must provide service, often in areas of need.

417. National Defense Education Act

If you become a full-time teacher in an elementary or secondary school that serves students from low-income families you can have a portion of your Perkins loans forgiven. Contact your school district's administration to see which schools qualify under this program.

418. Teacher Loan Cancellation

Teachers who work in low-income or subject matter shortage areas may have their loans cancelled or deferred. Perkins and Federal Direct loans can be cancelled or partially cancelled, and Federal Direct loans can be deferred.
Website: http://studentaid.ed.gov/PORTALSWebApp/students/english/teachercancel.jsp?tab=repaying

419. Child Care Provider Loan Cancellation

You may qualify for cancellation of a Federal Direct loan if you have a degree in early childhood education, are a childcare provider and work in a facility that serves low-income children.
Website: http://studentaid.ed.gov

420. Public Service Loan Forgiveness Program

You may have loans made through the Federal Direct Program forgiven if you work for any federal government, state government, local government or tribal government entity or most non-profit employers.
Website: http://studentaid.ed.gov

421. Law Loan Repayment Programs

There is a directory of loan repayment programs for lawyers who work in public service or underserved areas at the Equal Justice Works website at http://www.equaljusticeworks.org. The programs listed are sponsored by law schools, states and companies. Check if your law school participates in this program.

422. Business School Loan Forgiveness Programs

Some business graduate schools forgive loans for students who enter public service or non-profit careers. For example, Stanford University and Harvard University both offer loan forgiveness programs. Check with your business school's financial aid office. In addition, companies may provide this as a benefit, requiring you to commit to working a number of years with them.

423. Peace Corps

While the Peace Corps does not offer a loan forgiveness program, it offers several important educational benefits. With the Master's International Program, you can incorporate Peace Corps service into master's degree programs at more than 40 colleges and universities. Most schools provide students with opportunities for research or teaching assistantships, scholarships or a tuition waiver for the cost of credits earned while in the Peace Corps. The Fellows/USA Program offers volunteers who have returned home scholarships or reduced tuition in advanced-degree programs at more than 25 participating colleges and universities. Volunteers commit to work for two years in an underserved community as they pursue their graduate degree.

Website: http://www.peacecorps.gov

424.

Professional associations

Many professional associations offer loan forgiveness programs to help students who have recently entered the career. The Society of Automotive Engineers (http://www.sae.org), for example, offers the Doctoral Scholars Forgivable Loan Program, which can help repay your graduate school student loans. Take a look at the professional organizations listed in Chapter 2 or go to your library and check out the book *Encyclopedia of Associations.*

State Loan Forgiveness Programs

Many states offer loan forgiveness or scholarships for service as a way to entice students to work in underserved areas of the state or in fields with shortages. Some programs require that you are a resident of or attend a college or university in the state while others just require that you work in the state. Be sure to look not only at the state where you are a resident and will be attending college but also at all of the states where you might work after college.

425. Alabama
The Alabama Nursing Scholarship Program
Mathematics and Science Scholarship Program for Alabama Teachers
Website: http://www.ache.state.al.us

426. Alaska
Alaska Commission on Postsecondary Education Loan Forgiveness Programs for Teachers, Fisheries and Law Enforcement
Website: http://www.state.ak.us/acpe/

427. Arizona
The Arizona Loan Repayment Program for Health Professions
Website: http://www.hs.state.az.us/hsd/

428. Arkansas
The Minority Teachers Scholarship
Website: http://www.adhe.edu

The Rural Physician Incentive Program
Website: http://www.healthyarkansas.com

429. California
The State Loan Repayment Program for Health Professions
Website: http://www.oshpd.ca.gov/hwdd/slrp.html

Cal Grant T for Teachers
The Assumption Program of Loans for Education (APLE)
The Child Development Grant Program
The Graduate Assumption Program of Loans for Education
Website: http://www.csac.ca.gov

430. Colorado
Colorado Health Service Corps
Website: http://coloradohealthservicecorps.org

431. Connecticut
The Connecticut Minority Teacher Incentive Grant
Website: http://www.ctohe.org/sfa/

The Connecticut State Loan Repayment Program for Health Professions
Website: http://www.dph.state.ct.us

432. Delaware
The Delaware State Loan Repayment Program for Physicians and Dentists
Website: http://dhss.delaware.gov/dhcc/slrp.html

433. Florida
Critical Teacher Shortage Student Loan Forgiveness Program
Website: http://www.floridastudentfinancialaid.org

434. Georgia
The PROMISE Teacher Scholarship
The Service-Cancelable Federal Direct Loan for Health Professions
The Northeast Georgia Health System Service Cancelable Loan
The Registered Nurse Service-Cancelable Loan Program
*The North Georgia College and State University Military Scholarship
(National Guard)*
The Georgia Military College State Service Scholarship (National Guard)
The Georgia National Guard Service Cancelable Loan
*The Intellectual Capital Partnership Program (ICAPP) for High Tech
Professions*
The Scholarship For Engineering Education (SEE)
The HOPE Teacher Scholarship
The Osteopathic Medical Loan
Website: http://www.gsfc.org

435. Idaho
The Education Incentive Loan Forgiveness Program
Website: http://www.boardofed.idaho.gov

436. Illinois
Illinois Department of Public Health Medical Student Scholarship
Website: http://www.idph.state.il.us

437. Indiana

The Nursing Scholarship Fund Program
The Minority Teacher Scholarship
Website: http://www.in.gov/ssaci

438. Iowa

Primary Care Recruitment and Retention Endeavor (PRIMECARRE)
Website: http://idph.iowa.gov/ohds/rural-health-primary-care/primecarre

Teacher Shortage Forgivable Loans Program
The Nursing Education Forgivable Loan Program
Website: http://www.iowacollegeaid.org

439. Kansas

The Kansas Teacher Service Scholarship
The Nursing Scholarship
The Kansas Osteopathy Medical Service Scholarship
The Kansas Optometry Service Scholarship
The Kansas Dentistry Assistance
Website: http://www.kansasregents.org/scholarships_and_grants

University of Kansas Medical Center Loan Forgiveness Program
Website: http://ruralhealth.kumc.edu

440. Kentucky

The KHEAA Teacher Scholarship Program
The Early Childhood Development Scholarship
The Osteopathic Medicine Scholarship
Website: http://www.kheaa.com

441. Maine

Educators for Maine Program
Maine Access to Medical Education Program
Health Professions Loan Program
Maine Access to Veterinary Education Program
Dental Education Loan and Loan Repayment Program
Quality Child Care Education Scholarship
Website: http://www.famemaine.com

Maine Osteopathic Association Scholarships
Website: http://www.mainedo.org

442. Maryland

The Janet L. Hoffman Loan Assistance Repayment Program
The Loan Assistance Repayment Program–Primary Care Services
The Maryland Dent-Care Loan Assistance Repayment Program for Dentists
The Child Care Provider Scholarship
The Developmental Disabilities, Mental Health, Child Welfare and Juvenile Justice Workforce Tuition Assistance Program
The Distinguished Scholar Teacher Education Award
The Firefighter, Ambulance and Rescue Squad Member Tuition Reimbursement Program
The Maryland Teacher Scholarship
The Sharon Christa McAuliffe Memorial Teacher Education Award
The State Nursing Scholarship and Living Expenses Grant
The Physical and Occupational Therapists and Assistants Grant Program
Website: http://mhec.maryland.gov

443. Massachusetts

The State Loan Repayment Program for Health Professions
Website: http://www.state.ma.us

Tomorrow's Teachers Scholarship Program
Incentive Program for Aspiring Teachers Tuition Waiver
Website: http://www.osfa.mass.edu

444. Michigan

Michigan State Loan Repayment Program for Health Professions
Website: http://www.michigan.gov/mdch

Michigan Nursing Scholarship
Website: http://www.michigan.gov/mistudentaid/

445. Minnesota

The Minnesota State Loan Repayment Program for Health Professions
The Rural Physician Loan Forgiveness Program
The Urban Physician Loan Forgiveness Program
The Dentist Loan Forgiveness Program
The Rural Midlevel Practitioner Loan Forgiveness Program
The Nurses Who Practice in a Nursing Home or an ICFMR Loan Forgiveness Program
Website: http://www.health.state.mn.us

446. Mississippi
The Critical Needs Teacher Loan/Scholarship (CNTP)
The William Winter Teacher Scholar Loan (WWTS)
The Nursing Education Loan/Scholarship (NELS)
The Family Medical Education Loan/Scholarship
The Graduate and Professional Degree Scholarship for Health Professions
The Southern Regional Education Board Scholarship for Health Professions
The State Medical Education Loan/Scholarship
The State Dental Education Loan/Scholarship
Website: http://www.ihl.state.ms.us

447. Missouri
The Advantage Missouri Program for Business and Technology Fields
Website: http://www.dhe.mo.gov

The Missouri Teacher Education Scholarship Program and Minority Teaching Scholarship Program
Website: http://dese.mo.gov

The Physicians Student Loan Repayment Program and Missouri Nurse Loan Repayment Program
Website: http://www.dhss.mo.gov

448. Montana
The Rural Physician Incentive Program
Website: http://mus.edu/Prepare/Pay/Loans/MRPIP.asp

449. Nebraska
The Nebraska Loan Repayment Program for Health Professions
The Nebraska Student Loan Program for Medical Professions
Website: http://www.hhs.state.ne.us

450. Nevada
Nevada Health Service Corps
Website: http://medicine.nevada.edu/statewide/rural-health/health-service

451. New Hampshire
The New Hampshire Career Incentive Program for Education and Medical Professions
Website: http://www.state.nh.us/postsecondary

452. New Mexico
The Allied Health Student Loan-For-Service
The Medical Student Loan-For-Service
The Nursing Student Loan-For-Service
The Osteopathic Medical Student Loan-For-Service
The Health Professional Loan Repayment Program
The Minority and Women's Doctoral Assistance Loan-For-Service
The Southeastern New Mexico Teachers' Loan-For-Service
Website: http://www.nmche.org

453. New York
The NYS Regents Health Care Opportunity Scholarships
The New York State Regents Professional Opportunity Scholarships
Website: https://www.hesc.ny.gov

NYC Teaching Fellows
Website: http://www.nycteachingfellows.org

454. North Carolina
The NC Teaching Fellows Scholarship Program
The Master's Nurse Scholars Program (M-NSP) Graduate Program
The Nurse Scholars Program (NSP), Undergraduate Program
The Prospective Teacher Scholarships/Loans (PTSL)
The Teacher Assistant Scholarship Loan (TASL)
Website: http://www.cfnc.org

455. North Dakota
The Technology Occupations Student Loan Program
The Teacher Shortage Loan Forgiveness Program
Website: http://www.ndus.edu

The Physician State/Community Matching Loan Repayment Program
Dentist Loan Repayment Program
Long Term Care Nursing Scholarship and Loan Repayment Grant Program
Nurse Practitioners, Physician Assistants and Certified Nurse Midwives
State/Community Matching Loan Repayment Program
Website: http://www.health.state.nd.us

456. Ohio
The Nurse Education Assistance Loan Program (NEALP)
The Ohio Physician Loan Repayment Program (OPLRP)
Website: https://www.ohiohighered.org

457. Oklahoma

The Family Practice Resident Rural Scholarship Program
The Nursing Student Assistance Program
The Physician/Community Match Loan Program
The Rural Medical Education Scholarship Loan Program
Website: http://www.state.ok.us/~pmtc/

The Future Teachers Scholarship
The Teacher Shortage Employment Incentive Program (TSEIP)
Website: https://www.okhighered.org

458. Oregon

The Teacher Loan Forgiveness Program
The Rural Health Services (RHS) Program
Website: http://www.getcollegefunds.org

459. Pennsylvania

The Nursing Loan Forgiveness for Healthier Futures
The Agriculture Education Loan Forgiveness Program
Website: http://www.pheaa.org

Primary Care Practitioners Loan Repayment Program
The Private Practice Repayment Option (PPRO) for Health Professions
Website: http://www.dsf.health.state.pa.us/health/site/default.asp

460. Rhode Island

Rhode Island Department of Health (Health Professional Loan Repayment Program)
Website: http://health.ri.gov/programs/detail.php?pgm_id=179/

461. South Carolina

South Carolina Center for Teacher Recruitment
Website: http://www.scctr.org

462. South Dakota

South Dakota Department of Health (Health Professional Recruitment Incentive Program)
Website: https://doh.sd.gov

463. Tennessee

Minority Teaching Fellows Program
Tennessee Teaching Scholars Program
Website: http://www.state.tn.us/tsac/

Tennessee Department of Health (Health Access Incentive Program)
Website: http://www.state.tn.us/health/

464. Texas
The Teach for Texas Alternative Certification Conditional Grant Program (TFTACCG)
The Teach for Texas Conditional Grant Program (TFT)
The Train Our Teachers Award (TOT)
The Early Childhood Care Provider Student Loan Repayment Program (Early Childhood CPSLRP)
The Outstanding Rural Scholar Program (ORSP) for Health Professions
The Nursing Education Loan Repayment Program (NELRP)
The Dental Education Loan Repayment Program (DELRP)
The Physician Assistant Loan Reimbursement Program (PAL)
The Physician Education Loan Repayment Program Part III (Texas Family Practice Residency Training Program)
The Physician Education Loan Repayment Program Parts I and II (For Post Residency Practicing Physicians) (PELRP I and II)
The Professional Nurses' Student Loan Repayment Program
Website: http://www.collegefortexans.com

465. Utah
The Terrel H. Bell Teaching Incentive Loan (TIL)
Website: http://www.uheaa.org

The Utah Health Care Workforce Financial Assistance Program
The Nursing Education Loan Repayment Program (NELRP)
Website: http://health.utah.gov/primarycare/

466. Vermont
Vermont Area Health Education Center Program
Vermont Student Assistance Corporation
Website: http://healthvermont.gov/rural/programs.aspx

467. Virginia
The VDOT Engineering Scholarship Program
Website: http://www.virginiadot.org/jobs/engscholarprog.asp

The Nursing Scholarship Program
Website: http://www.vdh.virginia.gov/healthpolicy/primarycare/incentives/nursing/

The Virginia Teaching Scholarship Loan Program (VTSLP)
Website: http://www.doe.virginia.gov/teaching/financial_support/

The NHSC Virginia Loan Repayment Program
The Virginia Loan Repayment Program
The National Health Service Corp-Virginia Loan Repayment Program
(NHSC-VRLP)
The Virginia Loan Repayment Program for Health Professions
Website: http://www.vdh.state.va.us

468. Washington
Health Professional Loan Repayment
Washington Higher Education Coordinating Board for Health Professions
Website: http://www.wsac.wa.gov/health-professionals

469. West Virginia
The Medical Student Loan Program
Website: http://wvhepcnew.wvnet.edu or https://www.cfwv.com

470. Wisconsin
The Minority Teacher Loan Program
The Nursing Student Loan Program
The Teacher Education Loan Program
The Teacher of the Visually Impaired Loan Program
Website: http://heab.state.wi.us

Wisconsin's Health Professions Loan Assistance Program
Website: http://www.worh.org

471. Wyoming
University of Wyoming WWAMI Program for Medical Students
Website: http://www.uwyo.edu/wwami/

Military Education Benefits

Soldiering Your Way To An Education

The military has long provided many opportunities to get an education. Most of these opportunities are for service members and veterans. However, some are also for spouses and children.

All service members who were honorably discharged are eligible to receive a variety of educational benefits. And not all service has to be in the full-time, active-duty military. Some benefits are directed to those who serve part-time in the Reserves and National Guard.

Besides direct education benefits, the military also offers a variety of ways to earn college credit and even a degree. The Air Force, for example, runs its own community college system. All military servicemen and women are also eligible to take exams that help them earn college credit for the training and skills they learned while in

the military. By earning credit before you start school you can shave a semester or more from your program, which can save you hundreds or thousands of dollars.

Lastly there are special scholarships for service members. Some of these scholarships are also open to spouses. So even if you are not in the military but your spouse is you may apply for one of these scholarships.

So pay attention, soldier. You just might get your education for free.

Charles And Arthur's Story

Charles Mason, a sergeant major in the Army, is a self-described lifelong learner. However, it wasn't until this past fall that he finally received his master's of science in biotechnology management at the age of 44 from the University of Maryland University College.

Arthur Wilkinson, a command career counselor in the Navy, was a welder for 12 years before even considering joining the military or going back to school for an undergraduate degree. However, at the age of 35 he is well on his way to receiving his bachelor's of science in organizational leadership.

Both men were eager to earn degrees, all too aware of how important it will be when they retire from the military. More important, both men knew how to take advantage of their military benefits to help pay for their education.

Charles joined the military initially to receive money for college. "I ended up enjoying the Army so much I stayed for over 23 years," he explains. He says he took classes during most of that time. One of the main reasons Charles continually attended school, eventually earning his graduate degree, was for enhanced career opportunities and, he says, "to keep the gray matter active." His choice of a graduate degree also fit nicely with his work in the Army as a biomedical researcher.

Arthur returned to school to become more marketable for promotion while in the military and also to prepare himself for life after the Navy. Before he returned to school he was a Navy Counselor assigned to a ship. "Going to school was really burdensome," he explains. "Operational commitments didn't allow much time for formal classes." He says they were at sea a good deal of his three years abroad and otherwise were constantly training and preparing for deployment.

Both men used the opportunities provided by the military to defray the cost of their educations. When Charles joined the Army and began taking classes he only had to pay 25 percent of the cost. In graduate, school many of his classmates were fully funded by their employers. Fortunately, the recent GI Bill's "Top-Up" program has helped to equalize this situation and now Charles may receive 100 percent tuition assistance.

Arthur's education was fully paid for by the Navy in large part to his early planning. As soon as he got to basic training he signed up for the Montgomery GI Bill. The Navy deducted $100 per month for 12 months from his pay. He qualified for approximately $15,000 in tuition. With cost of living, that amount has risen significantly.

Both men agree that the Army and Navy education counselors do an excellent job. "They are very effective at their work," says Charles. Military benefits usually pay for 100 percent of tuition, but books and miscellaneous expenses are often not included. Charles suggests that soldiers use library copies of texts rather than purchasing them. "Who wants 500 pounds of outdated references cluttering up the house?" he asks.

For military students attempting to earn their degrees, completing classes can be time-consuming, requiring more than just average dedication. Charles says it is not for the impatient person. "You have to plan your curriculum carefully; you can't get all the classes you need everywhere." Taking classes while stationed overseas is another problem. "There are few opportunities for lab classes," he says "and virtually no opportunity for some of the upper-level labs."

Arthur adds to that, "Going to school and being in the military is a challenge. If assigned to a deployable unit, you cannot be sure of when you will have time to attend classes. Sailors usually roll to shore duty to complete their college educations, but even on shore we may be sent away for a variety of reasons."

Charles will retire next summer and approach the civilian world looking for employment. "I expect both my BS and my MS to be significant selling points in my resume," he says.

Arthur is not sure when he will retire from the Navy. He is certain, however, that his degree will help him both in the civilian workplace as well as make him a better officer while still in the Navy.

The Montgomery GI Bill

The Montgomery GI Bill–affectionately called MGIB–was signed into law on June 22, 1944, by President Franklin D. Roosevelt. Originally known at the "GI Bill of Rights," it provided a variety of educational benefits for returning veterans from World War II. Since then the bill has been amended several times and benefits have been expanded to not only help veterans return to civilian life but also as an incentive to encourage enlistment in today's all-volunteer military forces.

472. GI Bill–Active Duty
The GI Bill provides up to three years of education benefits for veterans for degree and certificate programs, flight training, apprenticeship, on-the-job training and correspondence courses. If you have served in the active-duty military you will need to take advantage of your GI Bill within 10 years of being discharged.
Website: http://www.gibill.va.gov

473. GI Bill–Selected Reserve
The MGIB for Selected Reserve covers the Army Reserve, Navy Reserve, Air Force Reserve, Marine Corps Reserve and Coast Guard Reserve, the Army National Guard and the Air National Guard. You must continue to serve in the Reserves during the time that you take advantage of the benefits.
Website: http://www.gibill.va.gov

474. GI Bill–Survivors' and Dependents' Educational Assistance Program (DEA)
The GI Bill provides what is known as the *Survivors' and Dependents' Educational Assistance Program (DEA)*, which gives up to 45 months of education benefits for eligible dependents of veterans who are permanently and totally disabled or who died while on active duty or as a result of a service-related condition.
Website: http://www.gibill.va.gov

475.

Veterans Educational Assistance Program (VEAP)

While in the military you can elect to participate in *VEAP*, which deducts money from your military pay for this program. Uncle Sam will match your contributions on a $2 for $1 basis. You can use this money for degree, certificate, correspondence, apprenticeship, on-the-job training programs and vocational flight training programs. You have 10 years to use your *VEAP* benefits and if you have money left over, your portion of the remaining contribution is refunded.
Website: http://www.gibill.va.gov

476.

State-sponsored National Guard benefits

As a member of the National Guard, you already qualify for the Montgomery GI Bill for Selected Reserve. Some states offer additional benefits. For example, the *Wisconsin Army National Guard Tuition Grant* provides up to eight semesters of full tuition benefits. You can even use your benefits at select schools outside of Wisconsin.

Get more information about your state's National Guard benefits by visiting these websites. For the Air National Guard visit http://www.ang.af.mil and for the Army National Guard visit https://www.nationalguard.com.

477.

Other state benefits

States also provide military benefits to active-duty, veteran and even dependents of service members. Check with your state's Department of Veterans' Affairs. Texas, for example, offers tuition waivers for veterans, which means if you were a Texas resident at the time you joined the military you may be exempt from having to pay tuition at public colleges and universities after you are discharged. A good resource is Military.com, which offers a summary of state benefits at http://www.military.com/benefits/veteran-state-benefits/state-veterans-benefits-directory.html.

478.

Enroll in a Servicemembers Opportunity College (SOC)

Being in the military can pose several challenges to getting your degree. You often have no control over your relocation from one base to another. You might get an assignment on a ship or at a base in a foreign country. You also receive specialized training that is not always recognized by colleges. To help you earn a degree, SOC was created and today is a consortium of more than 1,700 colleges and universities that provide educational opportunities for service members and their families.

The benefit is that by enrolling in an SOC-approved program, you can start or continue your education at military installations worldwide and SOC member colleges agree to accept each other's credits as transfer credits should you need to relocate and switch schools. If you are in an isolated location you can also take or continue your education through distance learning courses. Get more information at http://www.soc.aascu.org.

479.

Take all the free tests you can

You can earn college credit by passing special exams. While civilians must pay for each exam, as an active military serviceperson (or veteran) you can take these exams for free. Some of the free exams that you can take are the undergraduate-level Excelsior College Examinations, College Level Examination Program (CLEP) and the DANTES Subject Standardized Test (DSST). Contact your education officer or test control officer for more information. The DANTES (Defense

Activity for Non-Traditional Education Support) program administers examinations at more than 560 military installations to about 150,000 military personnel a year. Depending on your college, you can use your scores on DANTES tests to get credit. To learn more about the DANTES test program, visit http://www.dantes.doded.mil.

480.

Earn credit for your military training

Many colleges automatically give you course credit for your military service. Joliet Junior College in Illinois, for example, gives credit for physical education and biology to all members of the armed services. You may also be able to get additional credit for specialized training and education that you receive while in the military. For example, any College Level General or Subject Matter Tests taken at the United States Armed Forces Institute (USAFI) may count for credit.

To get credit for your military training, you need to provide documentation. Often this will come from one of the following sources:

481. Community College of the Air Force (CCAF)

The Air Force has taken a different approach to the education of its service members. It has established the Community College of the Air Force, which is made up of over 125 military schools and affiliated civilian institutions. The CCAF keeps a transcript for all students, and those who take enough courses and meet all requirements can earn an associate's degree in one of more than 65 areas in applied science. CCAF is open to all Air Force active duty, Air National Guard and Air Force Reserve Command personnel. The CCAF is a fully accredited college, and coursework along with degrees are accepted at most civilian colleges and universities. Since granting its first degree in 1977, the CCAF has given more than 237,000 associate degrees. Visit the CCAF website at http://www.au.af.mil/au/ccaf/.

482. Joint Services Transcript

One of the problems with earning credit for your military training is determining if it is equivalent to a college-level course and if so which one. To help sort things out the JST program was designed to eval-

uate the experience of service members for the purpose of granting college credit. While the individual college will decide whether or not to accept the JST recommendation for credit, the program has been widely adopted and is very helpful in allowing you to get credit for your military work.
Website: https://jst.doded.mil

483. Select a program that maximizes credit
Colleges typically require that you take 25 percent of your courses at their institution. However, different institutions have different policies for transfer credit. It's important to understand the requirements so you can select a program that will allow you to maximize credits from the JST program.

484. Save yourself a big headache by getting a copy of your VMET (Verification of Military Experience and Training) documents within 12 months of separation
Documentation of your military training can earn you college credits and save you money on tuition. Be sure to obtain your VMET documents within 12 months of your separation or 24 months of your retirement from the military. You can get your VMET papers at your transition support office.

Randall's Story

Randall Evans describes himself as a "39-year-old, active duty Chief Petty Officer of average intelligence, anticipating promotion to Chief Warrant Officer." His average intelligence includes an associate's degree from Central Texas College, a bachelor's degree in criminal justice from Columbia College and an expected master's degree in security management: industrial security at the American Military University. All this while he serves in the Coast Guard.

Randall is originally from Clearwater, Florida, but he and his family, a wife and two young daughters, currently live in Cape May, New Jersey, where he is assigned to the Coast Guard Investigative Service, Resident Agent Office. It is a job he has had for some time and one that he used his bachelor's degree to obtain. His current graduate study program will be an extension of criminal justice giving him new opportunities in the private security field.

Randall originally joined the Coast Guard when he was 20 years old and had 33 college credit hours. He seemed happy with where his education had taken him until eight years later he had an accident and found himself recovering from reconstructive knee surgery, facing a medical board and possibly being discharged from the service.

"I decided that having a bachelor's degree would pay more in the civilian sector than my monthly disability check," he says. So he started going to college at night and before long had an associate's degree and then a bachelor's degree.

Fortunately, Randall also received college credit from schools and course tests he had taken in the Coast Guard, reducing the number of classes he needed to complete his degree. "With nearly 19 years of service, my bachelor's degree definitely helped me to land my current job as a special agent with the Coast Guard Intelligence Service."

Randall knew however, that he wanted more. "I found it incredibly ignorant," he begins, "not to take advantage of the new Coast Guard 100 Percent Tuition Assistance program." If that weren't enough, "Some Coast Guard programs even pay for my books," Randall adds.

Randall is also able to attend a distant learning university. "The closest university is nearly two hours away, so taking advantage of distance learning is a vital option," he explains. He admits that making the decision to attend graduate school was hard because of the demands of his military career. However, his desire to excel got the best of him and he decided it was more important to make himself competitive in the job market. "Besides," he says, "I wanted to take advantage of the $10,000 in free education."

His only regret, he says, is that he did not have 100 percent of his bachelor's degree paid for through the military like he is doing with his graduate degree. He paid a substantial amount of money from his own pocket at Columbia College because at the time he was working on his undergraduate degree the military's tuition assistance program only paid $400 a quarter. Times have certainly changed, and Randall says now the Coast Guard Tuition Assistance program pays up to $750 per class, which is exactly what his classes cost at American Military University.

Randall says the process is incredibly easy. The education service officer gave him the paperwork, and he faxed it to the university. It has been so easy for him to utilize the military benefits offered through the Coast Guard that Randall encourages everyone to introduce themselves to the education service officer, find a degree path and go for it.

Randall says that when his superiors in the military found out he was attending graduate school many were impressed. "In another year I will have more education than my supervisors," he says. By the time Randall completes his graduate studies he will have three degrees, a military pension and 20 plus years of experience. He wholeheartedly encourages every Coast Guard member to take advantage of Tuition Assistance, but says jokingly, "Disclaimer: Individual results can be better than mine."

Special Military And Veteran Scholarships

Many veteran organizations provide scholarships to veterans, their spouses and dependents. Contact these organizations to see if they offer scholarships that apply to you and also get in touch with your local and state military and veteran organizations. You can find a good list of veteran associations, many of which offer scholarships, at the Department of Veterans Affairs website at http://www.va.gov/vso/.

Here are a few of the larger awards to get you started:

485. Air Force Aid Society
The *General Henry H. Arnold Education Grant* helps Air Force members and their families realize their academic goals. You must be dependent sons and daughters of Air Force members, spouses of active duty

members or surviving spouses of Air Force members who died while on active duty or in retired status.
Website: http://www.afas.org

486. American Veterans
The American Veterans provide scholarships to veterans who are members of the organization. The veteran's scholarships are $4,000 over four years.
Website: http://www.amvets.org

487. Armed Forces Communications and Electronics Association
This association offers several scholarships. The *AFCEA General Emmett Paige Scholarship* is for active-duty personnel in the uniformed military services, honorably discharged veterans or their spouses or dependents who are full-time students in an accredited four-year U.S. college or university. Applicants must major in electrical, computer, chemical or aerospace engineering, computer science, physics or mathematics. The *AFCEA Sgt. Jeannette L. Winters, USMC Memorial Scholarship* supports active-duty Marine Corps members or veterans. Applicants must be on active duty in the Marine Corps or honorably discharged and current undergraduates who are majoring in electrical, aerospace or computer engineering, computer science, physics or mathematics. Other undergraduate and graduate scholarships are also available from the association.
Website: http://www.afcea.org

488. Blinded Veterans Association
The *Kathern F. Gruber Scholarship Program* offers financial aid to the spouses and dependent children of blinded veterans. The veteran need not be a member of the Blinded Veterans Association but must be legally blind (either service-connected or not). Applicants must be accepted to or already be enrolled in a university or business, secretarial or vocational training school. There are eight scholarships worth $2,000 and eight scholarships worth $1,000.
Website: http://www.bva.org

489. Fleet Reserve Association
The Fleet Reserve Association provides scholarships to FRA members, honorary members and their dependents, spouses and grandchildren.
Website: http://www.fra.org

490. Foundation of the First Cavalry Division Association

The *First Cavalry Division Association Scholarship* is for the children and spouses of First Cavalry Division troopers who have died or become totally disabled while serving in the division. Active duty members of the division are also eligible.
Website: http://www.1cda.org

491. Military Chaplains Association

The Military Chaplains Association provides scholarships to seminary students who plan to become military chaplains. You must be a full-time student in an accredited seminary and currently approved as and serving as a chaplain candidate in the armed forces.
Website: http://www.mca-usa.org

492. Military Order of the Purple Heart

The *Military Order of the Purple Heart Scholarship* is for the children or grandchildren of a Purple Heart recipient or of a member in good standing with the organization.
Website: http://www.purpleheart.org

493. Navy-Marine Corps Relief Society

The *Admiral Mike Boorda Scholarship Program* helps eligible Navy and Marine Corps members pay for their postsecondary, technical or vocational education. Applicants must be active duty service members accepted to the Enlisted Commissioning Program, the Marine Enlisted Commissioning Education Program or the Medical Enlisted Commissioning Program.
Website: http://www.nmcrs.org

494. Navy Supply Corps Foundation

The foundation offers the *Navy Supply Corps Foundation Scholarship* to aid family members of foundation members and enlisted Navy personnel, including reservists and retirees. You must be a family member of a member of the Navy Supply Corps Foundation or an enlisted member, meaning active duty, reservist or retired.
Website: http://www.usnscf.com

495. Non-Commissioned Officers Association

The Non-Commissioned Officers Association offers scholarships to the spouses and children of its members. Children must be under the

age of 25 to receive a scholarship. There are four scholarships worth $900 for spouses.
Website: http://www.ncoausa.org

496. Paralyzed Veterans of America
The *PVA Educational Scholarship Program* offers scholarships to active life members of the Paralyzed Veterans Association and their immediate families for post-secondary education.
Website: http://www.pva.org

497. Seabee Memorial Scholarship Association
The *Seabee Memorial Scholarship* provides scholarships to the children and grandchildren of Seabees, both past and present. You must be the child, stepchild or grandchild of regular, reserve, retired or deceased officers or enlisted members who have served or are now serving with the Naval Construction Force or Naval Civil Engineer Corps, or who have served but have been honorably discharged. Scholarships are for four-year bachelor's degrees.
Website: http://www.seabee.org

498. Tailhook Association
The *Tailhook Educational Foundation Scholarship* assists members of and children of the members of the Navy's carrier aviation. Applicants must be high school graduates who are accepted at an undergraduate institution and are the natural or adopted children of current or former naval aviators, naval flight officers or naval aircrewmen. Applicants may also themselves be serving or have served on board an aircraft carrier in the ship's company or the air wing.
Website: http://www.tailhook.org

499. United Daughters of the Confederacy
The *United Daughters of the Confederacy Scholarship* supports lineal descendants of Confederate soldiers.
Website: http://www.hqudc.org

Can I go to college at the same time I am serving in the military?

One of the best ways to earn a degree while serving in the military is by looking online. Some programs require as few as a couple hours a day, and you can earn a bachelor's or master's degree online. It's important to check if you can use the GI Bill or Military Tuition Assistance at the college.

CHAPTER SIXTEEN

Avoid Financial Aid Scams

Keeping Your Money Safe

An important part of saving money for college is keeping your hard-earned cash out of the hands of scam artists. Recently, the Federal Trade Commission reported that there were over 175,000 incidents of financial aid scams, which cost consumers more than $25 million. This represents only the scams that were reported, and we've met hundreds of families that were taken for amounts from $20 to more than $1,000 who never reported the incident.

To keep your money safe you need to know what to watch out for in a scam. Most scams begin in the same way. An offer arrives in an official looking envelope from a company with an equally official sounding name. Inside you usually find a letter that appeals to your fear of how you are going to pay for college. Then comes an almost unbelievable offer. For a small sum of money this company will help you locate unclaimed scholarships, maximize your financial aid package and help you pay for college without any financial pain. It offers the answer you have been looking for and the price is peanuts compared to what you were planning to shell out for tuition.

If you send in a check you have probably just become another statistic for the Federal Trade Commission. We should point out that not all of these offers are illegal, which helps to explain why they exist year after year. But they certainly don't live up to their promises. Often what you get for your money is usually much less than you expected and certainly not worth your hard-earned money.

Arnold's Story

Like most adults going back to school, Arnold Breckenridge was overwhelmed by the cost. "There were all sorts of expenses, and not just from tuition. There were books, student fees and even an expensive parking permit. Plus, I would have to severely cut my hours at work," recalls Arnold.

While Arnold was determined to go back to school before he turned 40, which was only a year away, he still could not stop worrying about how to pay for it all. Then one day an innocent letter appeared in his mailbox inviting him to a seminar on paying for college.

"It looked like junk mail, but the opening paragraph caught my attention. It said that there were millions of dollars in unclaimed scholarships and billions of dollars in financial aid," he recalls. Arnold had not even begun to search for scholarships so he thought that it couldn't hurt to attend the free seminar.

"They get you when you are the most desperate. Even though I don't usually fall for infomercials I was desperate and rationalized that as long as the seminar was free and as long as I didn't buy anything I could at least get some free information" he says.

The seminar was held at a local hotel in one of the many bland-looking conference rooms. There were about 50 attendees like Arnold who sat and drank the free coffee and tea. Most were parents, but there were also a few adult students. Everyone had that same wearied look on their face.

"It was not a very pleasant sight. Everyone looked kind of depressed. But then again I was depressed just thinking of how much school was going to cost so I guess I too was one of those depressing faces," says Arnold.

The presenter that evening was just the opposite. Charming, funny and full of energy, this "expert" spoke for two hours about how much money was available to help parents and students. By the end of the seminar the crowd was smiling and laughing and everyone felt a new sense of hope that it just might be possible to pay for college without going bankrupt. The only catch was that to actually start getting the money the attendees would have to sign up for an $800 "counseling package" that included lists of scholarships and workbooks on getting financial aid.

"Again, I want everyone to know that I am a very skeptical person who does not buy stuff on late-night television," insists Arnold. "I even used to scold my mother, who would fall for those television shopping networks and order all kinds of useless stuff." But that night Arnold was a different person. "I thought to myself, tuition is going to cost me at least $10,000 over four years so spending $800 now is really not that much. Plus, as the presenter kept saying it was an 'investment' that would pay for itself many times over." That night Arnold waited in line with the other people to pay his $800 and the promise that in four to six weeks his problems would be solved.

"What I got for my money was useless," says Arnold plainly. He received a list of two-dozen scholarships. Most of them didn't even apply to him since he was an adult student. "It looked like it was just a photocopied list that was sent to everyone. The only 'customization' that I could see was my name at the top of the sheet."

Arnold also received several cheaply produced guides to applying for financial aid. But once he began to look into the financial aid process he found the same information for free on the Department of Education's website. Plus, he was able to get a financial aid officer at his school to help him with his forms. All for free.

"Basically I got ripped-off. There was nothing useful that I received. The company would not refund my money, and I really didn't have the resources to pursue it further. The only good that I hope comes from my wasted money is that my story prevents someone else who is desperate like me from making the same mistake," concludes Arnold.

500.

Avoid the common hooks of a scam

To keep your money safe, you need to understand the difference between what is promised and what you actually will receive. Let's take a look at how some of these scams work and why you should avoid them.

The promise: For a fee we will find "hidden" scholarships that nobody knows about. This virtually guarantees that you will be a winner.

The reality: For all practical purposes there is no such thing as a "hidden" scholarship. There are some obscure scholarships that have criteria that almost nobody can meet so they do go un-awarded. But chances are if 99.99 percent of students can't meet the criteria to enter then neither will you. All legitimate scholarships that have reasonable eligibility requirements are awarded. It is true that some have very few applicants, but these are not the awards that you will get. What you will typically receive is a generic list of scholarships that are anything but hidden or a list of scholarships that have such specific criteria that nobody can qualify.

The promise: To enter our mucho-money scholarship you must pay a tiny application fee. After all, what's $5 or $10 to enter if you can walk away with $1,000 or more in scholarships?

The reality: After paying the fee and sending in the application you'll get a nice card that says, "Sorry but you are not a winner." These companies count on tens of thousands of students sending in the application fee. Then even if they have to randomly award a $1,000 scholarship they still bank a huge sum of money from the fees. The defense against these kinds of fake scholarships is simple: Never pay an application fee. Real scholarships do not require any fee from applicants. Scholarship organizations, after all, are trying to give money away, not take it from those who apply. If a scholarship organization can't afford to process applications without a fee then they have no business giving away a scholarship.

The one exception is for a competition where it is more common to include a fee with your submission, but these are usually limited to musical or artistic compositions and performances. Plus, these competitions are not technically scholarships so our rule is still true: Never pay an entry or application fee for a scholarship.

The promise: You've won our scholarship! All we need is your credit card number to verify your eligibility so we can send you the money.

The reality: You'll get some unexpected and unwanted charges on your credit card. Never give out your credit card information to a scholarship organization.

The promise: We guarantee that you will win at least one scholarship!

The reality: There is no such thing as a guaranteed scholarship. Scholarships are competitive and by definition not every applicant will win. The only way you would have a "guaranteed win" is if you had to pay an entry fee and the prize you won was less than what you paid. We don't think any of you feel like paying $500 to be a guaranteed winner of a $100 scholarship.

The promise: For a fee we will help you complete the FAFSA application and submit it for you.

The reality: The full name of the FAFSA is the Free Application for Federal Student Aid. Notice how the word "free" is right there at the beginning. The FAFSA is designed to be completed by you. Now, this is not to say that it is easy. It is similar to doing your taxes and in fact much of the information from your 1040 will be used to complete the FAFSA. However, to pay a company a fee to complete your form is usually not a good idea since you will be providing them with all

---

Why do so many scammers succeed?

They feed on your fear of not being able to pay for college. A desperate person is much more likely to pay someone who promises an easy solution. To defend yourself you need to be aware of your emotional desire to find money as well as your logical side, which will alert you to a potential scam. Don't let your fears overcome your better judgment.

of the information you need for the forms anyway. All they do is fill in the numbers after you have done the hard work. A better option might be to use your tax planner or accountant. Since they have all of your pertinent information already, it should be easy for them to fill out the FAFSA.

The promise: Our researchers will put together a customized list of scholarships just for you.

The reality: You get a generic list of scholarships that you could have easily found on your own. You can find thousands of scholarships on your own in books and on the Internet without paying a search fee. Plus, you'll do a much better job.

The promise: Come to our free seminar to learn the secrets of going to college for free.

The reality: You get a sales pitch for any combination of the above. Not all seminars are scams or rip-offs, so you'll have to use your own judgment. However, one giveaway is if the seminar sounds like a sales pitch or contains promises that sound too good to be true. If you feel like the seminar is just a live version of a late-night infomercial, then you are probably looking at a seminar where you will be asked to part with your money for what may be totally worthless information.

501.

Know these red flags that indicate a scam

In general the major telltale sign that you are about to be taken by a dubious offer is if you are asked to pay any significant amount of money. Particularly if you are applying for a scholarship, never part with your money. Scholarships are meant to pay you money, not the other way around. Here are a few red flags to watch out for:

Red Flag: Registration, entry or administrative fee
Legitimate scholarship and financial aid programs do not require an upfront fee. Do not pay for anything more than the cost of postage.

Red Flag: Soliciting your credit card or bank account number
Never give out this kind of financial information to anyone who contacts you. The only reason someone would need this information is so that they can charge you.

Red Flag: Refusal to reveal name, address or phone number
You know that something is wrong when the person on the telephone won't reveal his or her name or contact information. All legitimate organizations have no problem giving you their appropriate contact information.

Double Red Flag: Guarantee
Remember, there is no such thing as a guaranteed scholarship in exchange for a fee. Legitimate scholarships are based on merit or need, not your willingness to pay a registration fee.

If you discover that you have been the victim of one of the scams above, don't be embarrassed. This happens to thousands of people every year. Report your experience to the Better Business Bureau and Federal Trade Commission (http://www.ftc.gov) to help prevent it from happening to others. Also, be sure to write us about it. We maintain lists of dishonest and worthless programs and would like to know if you encounter any new ones. The old adage of consumer protection applies to scholarships: "If an offer sounds too good to be true, it probably is."

CHAPTER
SEVENTEEN

You Can
Do It

You Can Do It!

Congratulations! You have reached the end of this book and now have the equivalent of a graduate degree in paying for college! As you read each of the 501 ways to pay for college we hope that you discovered some that are just right for your own situation.

Now that you know all of the ways that you can pay for college, it's time to put some of these methods to work. As you move into action, keep in mind that there is no "right" way to go about finding the money you need. By adding your own creativity and innovation to the knowledge that you have gained from this book, we are confident that you will find your own path to making college possible.

There will be times when you might ask, "Is all of this worth it?" Given the amount of sacrifices that you will be making it's natural that you'll question whether the reward is worth the price. To answer this question we felt it best to share with you the words of one of the students we interviewed for this book. Sally Stratton is 48 years old and after four years of struggle has just earned her first bachelor's degree. As you face the many challenges of going back to school, keep her words in mind whenever you find yourself questioning whether or not it is worth the effort.

Looking back it would be easy for me to say that returning to school at age 44 was no big deal. With my diploma now hanging on my wall it's tempting to forget all of the hardships that it took to get that piece of paper.

But I don't ever want to forget.

Getting my degree wasn't cheap and it wasn't ever easy. My family and I sacrificed a lot to make it possible. But through this difficult and arduous process I discovered something: the value of my education. I know how much my education truly costs—and it's a lot more than the dollars I paid for tuition. I actually feel sorry for some of my younger classmates who take the whole experience for granted and who will never know how valuable their education is.

I know that education is neither a right nor an entitlement. It is a choice and will only come to those who are willing to put in the work and tears to obtain it. But once acquired it can never be taken away. My education is priceless. My diploma now hangs in a place of honor. I am as proud of earning it as of anything else in my life. But it is because of the sacrifices that I had to endure that I cherish it so.

To the many adults who are just starting out on this journey I say, "Expect there to be challenges, assume the road will be rough, but at the same time welcome those same obstacles as a sign that what you are pursuing is of great value. Look into the mirror and yell, 'Bring it on!'"

We could not have said it any better. As you join the ranks of the thousands of adults who are successfully paying their way through college don't be afraid to take your future into your own hands. Always remember, there is no better investment that you can make than in your education.

We wish you the best!

Index